Provocative Business Change

Provocative Business Change

Business-Turfing

John A. Honeycutt

ISBN : 1-4196-1874-1

To order additional copies, please contact us.
BookSurge, LLC
www.booksurge.com
1-866-308-6235
orders@booksurge.com

Provocative Business Change

CONTENTS

This work is a product of many minds. There are a great many excellent books, publications, and other written sources that are baked into my understanding and beliefs of business change. Even more so, there are possibly hundreds of individuals who have influenced my learning through experience, debate, and teaching in the past twenty years. The firms I have worked for also provided solid guidance through innovative methodologies and mentorship. Additionally, the formal pursuits through Wichita State University, Houston Baptist University, and Cornell University have certainly influenced my thinking.

I am grateful for my mentors, friends, clients, colleagues, and family who have challenged my thinking and improved my understanding of this fascinating world. A special thank you is due to my editor, Robert R. Black, for his collaborative suggestions on this work. Thank you, Bob.

For the development and production of the book itself I feel a deep sense of gratitude:
- to the memory of my grandmother, Vera, for her example of love
- to my sister, Kerry and her family, for their encouragement over the years
- to my son, James, who blesses me with insightful conversation
- to my daughter, Danielle, who inspires me with her boldness and spunk
- to my beautiful wife, Jennifer, who awes me with her kindness and graceful spirit
- to my mother, Jody, who embodies all optimism
- And with special dedication to my father, V. A. "Bill" Honeycutt, because a wiser and better man than he, I'll never know.

Part 1

Introduction

Definition

Business-Turfing™. Metaphorical Verb: To landscape, reconstruct and generally improve an organization's business *terrain* during Provocative Business Change™.

Purpose of the Book

This book aims to improve the way business changes are managed, to improve the success rate of business changes, and, above all, to improve the most frequent type of business change—a *Provocative Business Change*™.

Provocative Business Change™ (PBC) serves to provoke, excite, or stimulate discussion, resistance and controversy. An estimated 75% of business projects, programs, and major initiatives each year in major organizations fit this category.

A PBC is one of several options taken to achieve a likely business benefit. A PBC tends to result in a fundamental change in the effectiveness or approach of the organization. A PBC might include, for example, process improvement, reengineering, supply chain initiatives, enterprise resource planning (ERP), customer relationship management (CRM), enterprise technology, Six-Sigma or quality projects, non-core outsourcing of information technology or business process functions, most marketing efforts, and many operations improvements.

Focus of the Book

This book focuses on business changes that have likely business benefit, but are only one of perhaps several dozen alternatives that *could-be* initiated for the intended benefit. Said anther way; these business changes are not *required* in the sense that the organization would go out of business if the project were not done. These changes are sometimes extremely important, and they might hold the promise of tremendous business benefit. Still, they are simply one alternative, or one set of several possible sets of alternatives. It is for this reason that they *provoke* excitement, resistance, and controversy within the walls of an organization.

Terrain

Figure 1 illustrates the scope of this book. Most business initiatives are well intended. Most have a reasonable possibility of financial benefit to the organization. Still, tens-of-thousands of well-intended PBCs (the type of change emphasized in this book) fail each year wasting time, effort, and money.

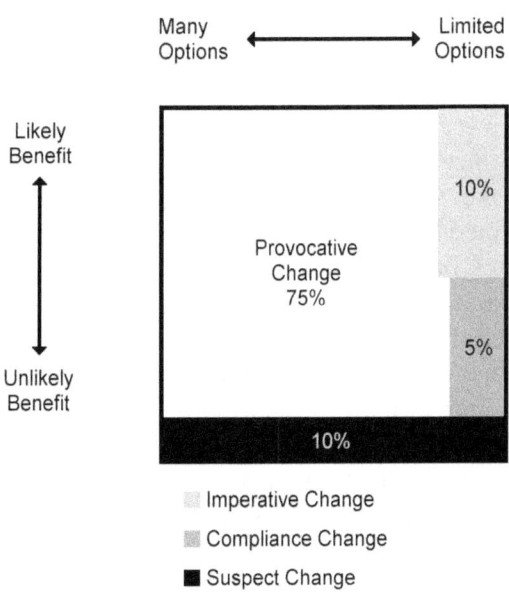

Figure 1: Scope of the book.

Imperative change is taken in order to survive in business; these changes account for perhaps 10% of changes within most major organizations. They are required for corporate survival and have a single, clear benefit to the business—to remain in business. Business imperatives are recognized by their sweeping impact on an organization, and typically have CEO-level sponsorship. Notably, most business changes that *claim* to be business imperatives are not really imperatives at all. Many of these would more accurately be categorized as a PBC. This book does not focus on business imperatives, but it will assist the reader in distinguishing a PBC disguised as a business imperative. Far too many initiatives are communicated as being imperatives. If this book serves only to influence more honest communication around a business change that is tempted to disguise itself as a corporate imperative, then the book will have served its purpose.

Compliance change is mandatory or required by business regulations; these changes account for about 5% of business changes in most organizations. These are required but have unlikely immediate business benefit. It is possible to reshape a compliance initiative into something that yields business benefit, but in most instances, organizations would not choose to pursue these efforts on their own. Many times these changes are very important, they might serve the interests of the community at-large, and they might absolutely be the right action to take. Still, they can be recognized by the absence of a clearly defined business benefit. Compliance efforts may stir-up resistance, but because they are truly required or mandated, the nature of resistance tends to be less caustic.

Suspect change tends to be discretionary and can be characterized as not having well defined business goals or business benefit. In an ideal situation, these changes would not be funded, and they would be shut down very early in the process. Most organizations have a process in-place to identify suspect projects, but somehow suspect projects get through the cracks even at the best companies. The best course of action for discretionary efforts with poorly defined business goals is to shut them down or defer them. This is easily said, and sometimes not so easily done. This book does not directly focus on how to deal with a suspect project, but many of the suggestions may assist a Change Agent to identify them and shut them down early. Depending on the maturity and rigor of an organization's business change process, up to 10% or more or its business changes may fall into this category.

Provocative change represents the most common business

change in most organizations today. These changes account for up to 75% of the budgeted project expenses in a fiscal year. They are sometimes broad and organization-wide, but they are often contained within one or two functions of the organization. Too frequently, a change of this type tries to communicate itself as being a business imperative—one that has clearly defined business benefit and is also *required* for corporate survival. These changes are provocative for several reasons—most significantly, often there are *winners and losers*. Even when everyone wins, some win more than others.

Part 2

Types of Business Change

Reasons initiatives fail widely vary. Business leaders and Change Agents too frequently blur the distinction between a likelihood of benefit and a requirement for a specific change. Figure 1 illustrates these separate ideas on separate axis. The variety of options and approaches possible to achieve business benefit is wide-open in most instances. True, there are some business imperatives where there are few options except to take a specific action. In the case of compliance, the number of options may also be limited. With those exceptions, most business change is not actually *required.*

That said, of course companies do need to adapt and change to keep pace—and eventually, without changing, some of these projects, programs, and major initiatives would become a requirement in the fullness of time. But they were not absolutely necessary at the time they were made.

The truth about most business changes is that they *might* yield a business benefit, but the initiative is not required for corporate survival and does not necessarily meet a regulatory compliance requirement. The initiative is not a business requirement; rather it is a *business option.*

This distinction of business benefit and business requirement blurs and projects fail to achieve their full potential. Employees hear how an initiative is presumably required when they believe or know that many other options also exist. They perceive the communication as "spin." They don't buy-into the idea and they may even put up roadblocks to its completion. Some employees, regrettably, might even celebrate the failure. This book assists the Change Agent and project team members in better identifying and addressing these issues.

More often though, project team members and impacted stakeholder groups make a valiant attempt to succeed, they are well intended, and they desire to achieve the benefits together. But full success is not obtained and the potential business benefit is marginalized. This book speaks directly to these situations. These are provocative situations where well-intended participants come together from Sales and Marketing, Information Technology, Finance, Operations, Human Resources and other functions. But roles, perspectives, and personal agendas make full success difficult.

This book introduces a straightforward framework improving the likelihood of achieving the full business benefit of a PBC. The framework has evolved over a twenty-year span of experience in working as an independent management consultant and as a leader in three large consulting organizations. This thinking represents experiences in working with over fifty Fortune 1000 companies, several privately held organizations, local governments, and international organizations based in China, Europe, Latin America and the United States.

Experienced change-agent practitioners will find the book's common sense framework to be a convenient reminder while working with a range of colleagues or clients. Newly minted consultants and service professionals will discover practical wisdom and suggestions that have proven to repeatedly work elsewhere. Project team members and those whose work group may be impacted by a pending change will become familiar with new points-of-view and acquire an improved method of communicating with and working with their colleagues.

- **Seasoned Change Agent:** Find convenient reminders and checklists.
- **Emerging Change Agent:** Find practical wisdom and considerations.
- **Business Change Participant:** Become familiar with alternate points of view.

Participants on a business change initiative tend to adopt one of three distinct perspectives this book calls Farmer, Scientist and Artist. The majority of this book is dedicated to exploring each of these perspectives or roles. By understanding the differences and interplay of the three perspectives, participants in a business change can more powerfully and more effectively work to achieve the business benefit.

Before examining the Farmer, Scientist and Artist roles, it is instructive to more deeply identify and confirm the type of business change. This book most directly applies to a PBC, and less directly applies to imperative, compliance, and suspect change. The section below completes the discussion of the four categories of business change.

Imperative Change

Business imperatives are required for the survival of an organization and always have a clearly defined benefit. Usually that benefit comes in the form of simply being able to stay in business. Less frequently they include step-changes required to begin a brand new way of doing business. A business imperative is distinguishable from a PBC by looking at the outcome or end-result. A business imperative can legitimately claim "if we don't take this action, we won't exist in the future."

Participating in or leading a business imperative has several advantages over a PBC. Business imperatives have very high-level senior executive sponsorship, and there is a compelling reason to move forward that can be crisply communicated. Employees recognize if they fail to get *on board* today, they may not have an employer tomorrow. This book offers techniques in making business imperative decisions, but they are secondary to the main thrust of the book, PBC.

Story: Defending Against Hostile Take-Over

With the reality of hostile corporate takeover attempts, most major organizations have plans in-place to fight off these uninvited events. When Computer Associates attempted to takeover CSC in the late 1990's, a company-wide initiative was set in motion to fend off the acquisition. Multi-faceted efforts to communicate with legislators, lawmakers, key clients, and employees in addition to coordination of management efforts around the globe were set into motion. Pro-active planning (including the need to fend-off hostile take-over attempts) may fall into the business imperative category.

Story: Unsolicited Acquisitions Efforts

Other more recent high profile deals include Comcast's $72 billion unsolicited acquisition of AT&T Broadband, Northrop Grumman Corp.'s $6 billion unsolicited bid for TRW, Inc., and Weyerhaeuser Co.'s successful $7.8 billion hostile acquisition of Willamette Industries. Regardless of whether attempted acquisitions are hostile, friendly, and successful or not, these activities will not disappear any time soon. They are part of the corporate landscape. When they turn up, they will get the highest priority from executive management, board involvement, and the investment community will respond.

Story: Airline's Struggle to Survive

A major airline was on the brink of financial disaster because their core customer, (the higher paying business passenger), was frustrated with frequent delays and inconsistent on-time arrivals/departures. The revenue loss was noticed by the stockholders and was reflected in the decreased stock price. The issue did not go unnoticed by executive management. The airline's situation elevated itself to business imperative—to substantially improve this key indicator (on-time arrivals) and gain back the customers. The airline succeeded in regaining much of its position, and improved its operations in the process by engaging the entire organization in a two-year initiative.

Initiatives like these examples make headlines, and deserve the attention they get. Even so, on a year-to-year basis, business change on this magnitude tends to be the exception, not the rule. Huge deals and large-scale corporate re-invention make the news but are not representative of the more frequent day-to-day changes most employees participate with. While cultural change and business strategy is the focus of many excellent business books and largely out of scope for this book, readers wanting to better understand these topics will find the Farmer section to be informative.

Business Imperative (for Survival) Examples
- Catastrophic response or avoidance
- Fending off hostile take-over
- Mergers and acquisitions
- Some safety initiatives
- Start-up businesses
- Some spin-offs

Compliance Change

Following the collapse of WorldCom and Enron, federal legislation responded—resulting in the Sarbanes-Oxley Act. Even Congressman Michael Oxley is reported to agree after-the-fact that a bit more flexibility for small—and medium-sized companies would have been a more appropriate solution. The impact of implementing financial and accounting controls to comply with the Act was broad sweeping. Some organizations and their stockholders no-doubt did find business value in the new controls. Many other organizations, (smaller organizations, for example), simply had to bear the expense in altering some processes to comply without any tangible return on their investment. It can be argued that business benefit arises from compliance change, but generally, regulatory requirements and other government-mandated programs do not have direct business benefit to the organization.

Story: Oil & Gas Regulatory Compliance

In major oil producing states and offshore in the Gulf of Mexico, the various oil & gas oversight bodies require each operating well site to be visibly inspected and reported as being inspected for leakage and other environmental issues on a daily or near-daily basis. The purpose of the requirement is to reduce potential environmental risks. Possibly, without the regulatory requirement, most oil and gas operating companies would still have inspections take place at the field level, but they would not choose to have the reporting requirements in-place that cause additional paperwork for the headquarters. Changes to the reporting requirements must be complied with, but may not have direct business benefit to the operating companies.

Within the Human Resources function of most all organizations, HR professionals must be familiar with the layers of employee rights. This includes laws, court rulings, and agreements influencing employer-employee relations. For example, the Family Medical Leave Act (FMLA), the Fair Labor Standards Act (FLSA), the Occupational Safety and Health Act of 1970 (OSHA), the National Labor Relations Act (NLRA) all come into play. Compliance is not optional, but in many instances there is not a direct return on investment to the business for instituting new rules or policies to comply.

Actions an organization might take on a compliance project for a mandatory required project can be assisted by some of the techniques in this book, but they are incidental to the chief purpose of the book. Participants with a compliance project or program will find the Scientist section to be the most relevant.

Compliance (or Mandatory) Examples
- Legacy contract fulfillment
- Regulatory compliance
- Many HR initiatives
- Sarbanes-Oxley

Suspect Change

Suspect or discretionary changes made in a business usually have unlikely or ill-defined business benefit, and the changes are not actually required to be made. The reader can identify a suspect change by the absence of clearly defined objectives and tangible business results.

Both the Farmer and Scientist sections in this book are useful in identifying a suspect business change. In some instances, a suspect change can be transformed into a PBC (one with likely business benefit) by prudently applying the better practices outlined in these two sections.

Examples of suspect projects include those done because a manager has not used up allotted funds in the general operation of the business. Managers fear they will lose budget allotments for the coming year if the money is not spent on something...anything. Sometimes suspect business changes are pet projects of a person in authority. Sometimes, they simply mask an attempt to solve a political feud.

In government, our lawmakers sometimes call suspect change a pork barrel project. Some research and development (R&D) projects fall into this bucket.

Story: Poorly Formulated Internet Initiatives

At one of the largest utility companies in the United States, a mid-level manager initiated three Internet projects. All three projects made it through the first round of screening and appeared on the list of planned projects. Each week, a considerable amount of discussion was spent on the three projects, with very little movement forward. The ideas were conceptually interesting, and possibly could have yielded business benefit, but they were poorly formulated beyond the concept level, and had no real executive sponsorship. Eventually, all three were appropriately shut down or refashioned, but not before several months had passed and tens of thousands of dollars wasted in employee time and vendor expense.

Story: Attempt to Use Technology to Solve a Political Issue

At a top-five technology manufacturer, a Director had engaged two consulting firms to build a custom application to assist in resource leveling the company's distributed engineering capability. A million dollars had been allocated and tentatively approved. Fortunately, in the first few days of deeper analysis, the root issue became apparent. A new computer application was not needed, rather one of the business leaders at one of the larger remote facilities held his information close to the vest, and did not willingly share business forecasts with the headquarters staff. An executive intervened and appropriately clarified the need (and requirement) for all facilities to share and report their forecasts. In this instance, the Director at headquarters wrongly attempted to create a business change to solve a political issue.

Projects like these are becoming rare with increased emphasis on initiatives like Six-Sigma and Capability Maturity Model® Integration methods. Still, they drain resources and money.

In the examples sited, the web manager viewed his world as an "Artist." He would have been well served to have better understood the role of "Farmer" and "Scientist" and incorporated those viewpoints into his efforts. The computer-manufacturing director attempted to solve her communication issues with her peer through a very expensive (and likely to fail) business change. By taking a Farmer perspective, this otherwise costly initiative was correctly thwarted by the executive before too much time, effort, and money was invested.

Ideally, the suspect project will be shut down early in the process, or re-shaped to have defined business benefit so that there is no cost sunk in pursuing it. In this book, there are a few tips and techniques on how to identify and stop a suspect project. The Farmer and Scientist sections help identify suspect business change.

Suspect (or Discretionary) Examples
- "Use it or lose it" budgets
- Pet projects of leaders
- Political feud
- Some R&D
- Pork Barrel

Provocative Change

These business changes are the focus of the book. Let's take a closer look the meaning of a Provocative Business Change™. The word "provocative" is synonymous with challenging, stimulating, and exciting. But it is also synonymous with insulting, confrontational, or even inflammatory. Depending on which end of the change you might be on, the vantage point can be either of these extremes.

Even a low profile, humdrum project is going to be offensive to someone, if it encroaches on turf, or if it is confusing or going to disrupt something that others are proud of.

Story: Pride of Ownership Gets In the Way of Improvement

One of the largest court-reporting firms in the United States had a particular form each court reporter/stenographer was required to complete when submitting their work. The manual form was cumbersome and outdated, requiring a traditional typewriter rather than the PC technology each of the court reporters used on their jobs. In this small example, the provocative nature of the potential improvements never got a chance to be discussed. Why? The person in charge of filing the forms designed the original form and was very proud of them, she did not understand technology, and she did not want to change her comfortable methods.

Story: Best-of-Breed versus Enterprise-wide Philosophy

One of the top building and construction firms in North America chose a "best-of-breed" approach to its technology when a majority of other organizations of its size in most industry segments pursued an enterprise-wide application suite. The choice to go "best-of-breed" clearly lined up with this organization's hands-off approach to running the various business lines. The benefit includes higher degrees of flexibility within the business lines, but required extra effort at the corporate level to leverage economies of scale and scope. This was not the easiest and most convenient approach for the centralized shared services organizations, such as the corporate Finance.

In contrast, a county government in California pursued a countywide implementation of Finance and Accounting and Human Resources technology to cover all 17,000 county employees. The standardization allowed for lower total operating cost, but required compromise and adaptation of common business processes in otherwise different county organizations. This approach promised cost savings to the tax-payers, but introduced uncomfortable process changes for many of the county agencies.

In the construction firm and county government illustrations, neither approach was fully right or wrong. Either organization could have chosen to be best-of-breed or enterprise-wide. It is for this reason that the business changes were provocative. Distributed versus centralized is not a new concept. The choice of distributed or centralization has and will continue to introduce many PBCs.

PBCs comprise about 75 percent of most business changes (planned line-item project expenses) inside large organizations in the United States. These include changes made in process improvement, reengineering, supply chain initiatives, ERP, customer relationship management, enterprise technology, Six-Sigma or quality projects, non-core outsourcing of information technology (IT) or business process functions, some marketing efforts, and even operations improvements.

This book offers essential ideas to improve the success rate and degree of success during PBC.

PBC Examples
- ERP/CRM/enterprise technology
- Six-Sigma or quality projects
- Operations improvements
- Supply chain initiatives
- Many marketing efforts
- Non-core outsourcing
- BPI/reengineering

Part 3

Roles and Perspectives

This book serves several reading styles. Some readers will find value in skimming through major sections, internalizing the broad points. Some readers will find a cover-to-cover approach to work best. Regardless of the approach to reading and using the book, ideally, three players in essential roles will review this book and discuss the contents before moving forward with a project.

- Executive sponsor
- Project manager
- Business practitioner

Other corporate personnel can also benefit by reading and then discussing the concepts and tactics addressed in this book. A broader audience includes:

- Management consulting firm account executive
- Corporate Communications team member
- Project team subject matter expert (SME)
- Project team business analyst
- Training team member
- Project team leader
- HR team member
- IT team member
- Other leader

The basic structure of this book is built around three roles played metaphorically by participants in a business change. An exceptionally done business change will incorporate these three separate roles. The paradigms illustrate and honor all three points of view equally.

- **The Farmer** has a unique general overview of what runs the business and what business changes need to be made. His or her areas or scope of interest are opportunity, obligation, objectives, outcome, and order.
- **The Scientist** has a unique perspective of business practices and knows how to operate the business on a day-to-day basis and how specific changes can help the business. His or her areas or scope of interest are plan, problem, process, prototype, and prudence.
- **The Artist** has a unique perspective of the people who make up the business. He or she will frequently have an explicitly creative role in the organization, or will have a business

strategy, or organization change management perspective. His or her areas or scope of interest are culture, communication, creativity, capability, and core HR.

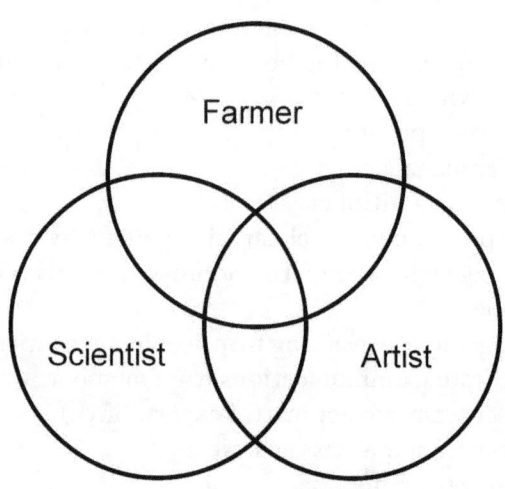

Figure 2: The three primary roles.

Thus, the Farmer, the Scientist, and the Artist incorporate the three various aspects or qualities of the central, primary figures who must make PBCs.

There is a Generalized Perspective for Each Role:
- **Farmer**—overview (what)
- **Scientist**—practices (how and when)
- **Artist**—consideration (who and why)

There are Five Areas of Interest for Each Role:
- **Farmer**—opportunity, obligation, objectives, outcome, order
- **Scientist**—plan, problems, process, prototype, prudence
- **Artist**—culture, communication, creativity, capability, core HR

Examples Help Illustrate the Differences:
On a farm, when a fence is broken:

- A farmer attends to practical, operational matters: the fence needs fixed, so fix the fence.
- A scientist approaches the issue through measurement and plans. How much labor and materials are needed to fix the fence? When does this need to be completed?
- An artist considers the possibilities. Who is interested in this fence? Why might they be interested?

In a lab, when a laboratory experiment is conducted:

- A farmer will observe and appreciate an overview, perhaps even be intrigued, with the outcome of the experiment, but will not necessarily be interested in the details. What is the purpose of the experiment? What does it mean?
- A scientist is "in the zone" during this event. A laboratory offers instruments to measure and monitor with controlled adjustments made at the right time. Through a specific process, data is captured and conclusions are drawn.
- An artist might be intrigued by the relationship of the equipment and the environment. An artist may be curious about why the scientist cares about the experiment, but be less interested in the experiment itself. Why does the scientist care about the experiment?

In a studio, when a painting is in process:

- A farmer would recognize the tools of the trade and appreciate the tools. A farmer might also know how to use the tools — but more for function rather than for creation. What can be accomplished with the tools?
- A scientist might very well wonder how the process of making a painting could be replicated or made routine—almost removing the creativity out of the process and making the process repeatable and predictable. How can the process be streamlined and improved?
- An artist would feel at home and possibly begin to start a particular project, and then set it aside for even days at a time while starting other projects and ideas. Some ideas may never get finished, while others are completed with incredible speed.

Using the farm, the lab, and the studio as backdrops for exploring the three basic roles in a business change is instructive. Each role is most comfortable in its own domain. While in another domain, the roles are able to function, but they tend to remain within their particular point-of-view rather than adapting to the situation at hand. This is neither good nor bad. It is simply a general truth.

Business Examples Help Further Contrast the Differences:

Theses illustrations describe business initiatives, whereas the issues pose similar differences in viewpoints:

With a new marketing initiative, when project communication is broken:

- The Business Farmer wants the communication to get fixed. What needs to be communicated? What business opportunities are being lost?
- The Business Scientist wants to estimate and plan the communication requirements. How will communication be produced, and when will it be distributed?
- The Business Artist identifies who the stakeholders are and what their interests and communication needs are. Who needs the communication, and why do they need it?

In a call center, when customer service scores are lower than expected:

- The Business Farmer wants the customer service to improve and the complaints to go down. What are the business implications of poor customer service?
- The Business Scientist wants to identify metrics to measure different aspects of customer service and plan improvements. How can the customer service be improved? How frequent are the complaints?
- The Business Artist explores why the customer dislikes the service and how service might be re-invented. Who are the customers? Why do they become frustrated? Who else is involved in servicing our customers?

During a business process improvement effort, before any decisions about the design get finalized:

- The Business Farmer wants to hear what the organization is doing compared to industry benchmarks. What does this organization look like in comparison to competitors?
- The Business Scientist wants to breakdown each piece of the value chain, analyzing the processes and estimating how improvements might impact the metrics. How can the process be refined in the most efficient and effective way?
- The Business Artist looks for alliances outside the organization—or alternatively, inward for who has competency inside the organization for new approaches to explore. Who should become a partner or alliance? Why are things done they way they have always been done?

It is a fundamental premise of this book that all three viewpoints are valid. An excellent management program for business change balances these viewpoints. Over-reliance on one viewpoint results in frustration or even failure. Further, the executive sponsor, program manager, and business change practitioner should each incorporate a little farming, science, and art into the way they approach the overall effort.

Poorly designed and executed programs fail to incorporate at least one of these roles, or paradigms (Farmer, Scientist, and Artist). In other instances, the programs do include each of the three roles, but individuals filling those roles don't sufficiently understand the importance of their colleague's viewpoints or language.

Each Role has a Primary Recommendation:

In addition to describing each of the three roles, this book offers one primary recommendation to each role. The recommendations summarized here are illustrated and clarified in their respective sections:

- **Farmer**—"Get in the wheelbarrow."
- **Scientist**—"Reduce or eliminate jargon."
- **Artist**—"Speak about actions and concrete results."

This book directs its approach to the use of metaphorical roles played by people—by Business Farmers, Business Scientists, and Business Artists in an organization. PBCs in a good organization are made from the balanced deliberations of all three.

Many large-scale business transformation efforts have dramatically failed because one of these perspectives is over-emphasized. Smaller projects fizzle and do not produce powerful business results for the same reason. All change participants need to acknowledge the validity of each perspective. Change Agents ideally understand each role. The best Change Agents are able to alter their perspective at will during discussions and interactions with other participants.

Part 4

Farmer

Being a Farmer

"Great innovations should not be forced upon slender majorities." Thomas Jefferson, 1808.

"Controversial proposals, once accepted, soon become hallowed." Dean Acheson, 1962.

Any given individual working on a business change may have an affinity toward the role of Farmer. Also, there are several job titles that tend to require those occupying the title to serve as a Farmer. A list of job titles is presented to illustrate those who are most typically acting as a Farmer on a business change.

- Operations Management
- Business Executive
- Account Executive
- Business Leader

Business Farmers focus on the Five-Os: Opportunities, Obligations, Objectives, Outcomes, and Order.

I grew up in a Kansas farming community. We had cattle and horses. I saw as a young boy that my father was very practical and straightforward. He looked at the big picture.

A farmer will attend to practical matters and will set priorities, watch the seasons, the production, growth, conservation, and use of resources. Executive management will behave similarly to a farmer by weighing the pros and cons of taking an action or not taking an action, of dealing mainly with the cause and effect of running the business.

So in this role as Business Farmer, business change participants look at running the business from unique points of view. There are five areas comprising that point of view: opportunity, obligation, objectives, outcome, and order. A Business Farmer thinks in terms of taking advantage of the opportunity. Before moving forward with an initiative, they know overarching issues and have a vision for where the initiative might lead.

Sponsorship and Commitment

Leadership, sponsorship, and executive commitment are essential motivational factors in any business. Executive commitment does nothing more than express sound leadership. It says to all others in the business, "Follow me," like the famous statement of the Army officer whose statue is at the gates of Ft. Benning. No good executives would ask of others what they themselves would not do.

Story: Get in the Wheelbarrow

In the summer of 1860, as a myth-like story is told, Jean Francois Gravelot (better known as "The Great Blondin") walked across Niagara Falls on a tightrope as a publicity stunt. For the crossing, Blondin stretched a 1,100 foot long—3 inch diameter manila rope from what is now Prospect Park in Niagara Falls, New York to what is now Oakes Garden in Niagara Falls, Ontario. Huge crowds gathered to watch on both sides. Thousands showed up to see him try this feat. Blondin began carefully and deliberately. He put one foot and then the other on the tightrope and began to walk across, inch-by-inch, step-by-step. When he got to the middle, everyone knew that he was as close to the end as to the beginning. If he made one false step, he might slip and drown. Blondin proceeded with care and determination and got safely to the other side. The crowd went wild. They shouted and yelled and cheered his courage and skill. But Blondin said, "I'm going to do it again." So he did it again, and again the crowds loved him for it.

Then, after walking across several times, Blondin said, "This time I'm going across pushing a wheelbarrow full of dirt." The crowd could not believe what they heard. Blondin loaded a wheelbarrow with dirt and proceeded across the tight rope just as he done on previous crossings. Slowly pushing the wheelbarrow, he got to the other side. He continued nine or ten more times.

On the last time trip across, a man yelled out, "Mr. Blondin, I believe you could do that all day." When Blondin heard this, he dumped out the dirt and said, "Get into the wheelbarrow." The man was shocked at the idea of being asked to do such a thing and quietly withdrew from the crowd, unwilling to back up his words of praise and support with any commitment of his own.

So the moral here is that sometimes people will sponsor a project, but they will not take the risk themselves to support the project, to get in the wheelbarrow. They think it's a good idea, they want to watch it happen, and they get entertained by launching projects, but they will not take a risk themselves to see that the project succeeds. For executives, account executives, and business leaders who are sponsoring a business change, the primary moral here is to *get into the wheelbarrow* if you really do believe in the initiative.

Story: Build Your House on the Work Site

A similar story is told about E.I. Du Pont. Du Pont moved to America as a young man after serving as an apprentice to Antoine Lavoisier, chief of the French gunpowder works at Essone (and founder of modern chemistry). The Du Pont family emigrated from France in the early nineteenth century. Du Pont saw the poor quality of gunpowder being used by the American riflemen and put his expertise to work to improve the quality. In 1802 he began building a mill along the Brandywine River. Du Pont notified his family-friend, President Thomas Jefferson, and soon received U.S. Army contracts for refining saltpeter, followed by substantial orders for gunpowder from hunters. Brandywine River Powder Mills produced its first gunpowder in 1803.

Du Pont's Brandywine gunpowder complex was housed in separate buildings, which contained the various stages of production—stamping mills, rolling mills, grain mills, glaze mills, machine shops, and power house. Machinists and millwrights, the precursors of mechanical engineers built the complex. Steam engines drove conveyor belts that moved materials along the production lines. Du Pont's were the largest powder mills of the time and were unique in that they made gunpowder to the specification of the consumer.

Du Pont also instituted management practices that established safety practices and ensured high-quality production. However, these practices lacked one critical initiative that drew criticism from the townspeople and workers alike. They were afraid that Du Pont was just saying his complex was safe and would not explode when he in fact did not mean it. They thought that they were at risk—their very lives— while management was not.

Du Pont addressed the problem. He built his house on the work site. He moved his family into a house adjacent to the plants where the gunpowder was being refined, so that if an explosion occurred, he and his family also would be at risk, injured or perhaps even killed.

This story of Du Pont provides a moral with business applications. In a business change, when it is clearly evident that the executive sponsor himself is at risk for failure, such a business commitment is infectious and will get people on board. This kind of dramatic commitment to provocative initiatives may seem unnecessary to some executives. Regrettably, we need not be reminded that failed businesses are full of stories of executives who have sat back while others take the risks.

Story: In a Heartbeat I Would

Another business story that demonstrates the value of personal executive commitment arises from my own experiences. It also dramatically illustrates an aspect of business commitment toward an initiative: mutual advantage or plain old good business sense.

I had the pleasure of working with an account executive at a large management and consulting firm. Dan was stumped because his client had spent several million dollars in consulting fees with his organization but was initially balking at a $150,000 business-to-business web application. Over lunch I posed a straightforward question. "Dan, if it were your own $150,000 out-of-pocket cost, would you invest in the web application?" And he looked me square in the eye and said, "In a heartbeat I would."

Dan really believed in the initiative, so my advice was simply to get approval for his own company to pay for it and give it to the client for free in return for receiving any future benefit accrued by his client, or at least part of the benefits that would result from use of the web application.

He did just that. That week his client contracted with Dan's firm to invest in the new web application, paying for all the consulting fees rather than having it done for free and splitting the revenue. It was Dan's confidence which caused his client to take him up on his proposal, not just the prospect of getting something free. Dan's confidence about his own product convinced them to accept an initiative in which both companies benefited.

In this example, similar to the other two stories, when the sponsor saw the consulting firm was willing to put some skin in the game, the signed contract came much easier to acquire.

Opportunity

Decreased cost and increased revenue, these are the most basic interests of a Farmer.

The initial area of interest for the businessman or businesswoman in the role of the Farmer is opportunity. "He who hesitates is lost." The old clichés ring true when it comes to knowing when opportunity knocks. To wait until it is too late can bring tragic results. The Farmer in our business model knows that, and he or she is quick to respond to good, reasonable chances that can increase profit.

Opportunity is the number one business priority from the Farmer's point of view. Scientists and Artists must learn to think in terms of opportunity to work well with the Farmer, and the Farmer must be able to convey a sense of opportunity to them as well.

Story: Five-Year Opportunity Plan

A billion-dollar wanted to grow. The company needed a five-year growth plan. The CEO, COO, and senior leadership all knew that they had an opportunity to expand even though they were already the largest in their industry. They had an opportunity possibly even to double their revenue within a five-year period, but they needed a road map. That is, they knew what they were; where the opportunities were; and needed only a business guide to go directly to the opportunities in the quickest and most profitable manner.

The road map they devised took into account their core business, their competitors, suppliers, and business partners. Their internal operations, including people, process, and technology, were all evaluated. By the fifth year of implementing their plan, they had realized their growth aspirations. Without the opportunity plan, such aggressive growth would have been difficult at best.

Story: Defining the Opportunity

Without first clearly identifying the opportunity to be pursued, a major grocery retailer enlisted a consulting company to propose a project. The request was not coherently defined among the retail organization's business leaders.

The consulting firm assembled a group of 20 of the grocer's representatives, including top management. The firm fashioned a list of six possibilities. The list ranged from making a supply chain plan to a warehouse improvement effort. Some items on the list emphasized reaching new market segments and introducing new product lines. Other items on the list emphasized improved operations, and streamlined processes to yield reduced cost. Each of the 20 people indicated their viewpoint of where the proposed effort should focus.

With all viewpoints tallied, it became quite clear that nothing was clear. While all participants agreed that something needed done, his or her perspective greatly varied, even among the executives. In the end, the consulting firm advised starting with a strategic alignment study to better define the opportunity.

These stories illustrate that a clear definition of the opportunity on the front end, especially with regard to executive alignment to get sponsorship, is essential to the success of an enterprise. All too often in large organizations, one business leader will launch an initiative that sounds familiar enough to other business leaders that the other leaders think they understand the initiative being proposed. Gertrude Stein was asked on her deathbed, "What is the answer?" She faintly replied, "What is the question?"

Here is an outline of four things the Farmer does to take advantage of business opportunity. Each is discussed within a framework of overview, considerations, and practices:

- Prepare the Team
- Make a Vision Statement
- Find Business Opportunity
- Promote the Project

⏺

Prepare the Team

Overview: Prepare selected business participants and project team members in the use of a structured transition framework. Transition leaders and team members are prepared to lead change efforts. If a consulting organization is enlisted to work with the team members, the firm's methodology should be used to train team members.

Considerations: For large initiatives, training is highly recommended for key team members. All transition team members should be exposed to general "change" concepts. For large-scale initiatives, active engagement by experienced transformation practitioners is important. Who should be on the team? Are there some who do not need to be on the initial team, but may be important later?

Practices:

- Identify Change Agents (Change Agents are described in Part 8 of this book) and form a team.
- Identify skill gaps with business personnel and project staff.
- Gather training material available to address the gaps (use the consulting firm's methodology if a firm is engaged).
- Identify a methodology to use, and discuss how to best use it.
- Create an electronic filing and tracking system for the effort. (Web-based collaboration tools are becoming increasingly useful for this purpose).
- Distribute basic information and training to team members.
- Conduct brainstorm session with team about how best to organize the work.
- Conduct a status meeting with executive management prior to a more robust launch of the effort.

Make a Vision Statement

Overview: The vision statement should be aspirational, achievable, and paint a clear picture of what the organization hopes to achieve by taking advantage of the business opportunity. A clear vision statement serves as the starting point for future communication. It remains a continuous reference point for decisions as they are made.

Considerations: Any level within the organization can contribute toward making a vision statement, but any such level should include a cross-section of stakeholders who are sufficiently familiar with the business opportunity being sought. Management need not exclusively draft a vision statement. To that extent, leaders should enlist contributions from lower levels of employees within the organization who may see the business opportunity from a unique perspective. Why should this initiative be done? Who will benefit if this is initiative is successful? Who might be a good facilitator for this visioning exercise?

Most of us are familiar with the story of the blind tribesmen who touched an elephant. The one who touched only the tail thought the elephant was a rope; the one who touched only the elephant's side thought it was a wall; the one who touched its leg thought it was a tree, and so forth. The principal of combined contributions runs throughout the art of making good business decisions. Every good Farmer wants "to hear from" those the Farmer can identify as likely to have good ideas, no matter where that person is on the corporate ladder. Major initiatives can benefit enormously from vision statements drafted with the help of lower agents within the organization.

Practices:

- Review any existing organization vision, strategy, and brand visions.
- Enlist a skilled facilitator to conduct the visioning session.
- Form a team of six to ten visionary people from various levels of operation.
- Include a cross-section of experts and management.
- Distribute copies of information a few days prior to the session.
- Conduct brain-storming visioning session (2-4 hours minimum; 2-3 days maximum in the rarest of situations).
- Reach agreement on the general content—not specific phrasing.
- Verify content is aspirational, achievable, and goal oriented.
- Verify that content is consistent with the organization's larger visions of operation.
- Draft three or four versions (styles) using the content from the group.
- Distribute findings to the team; reach consensus for one version.

❧

Find Business Opportunity

Overview: Business opportunities, in their most basic form, are either decreases in cost or increases in revenue. Opportunities may include streamlining an existing process, restructuring the sequence of an existing process, or eliminating a process that is no longer needed. Other opportunities include expanding into new markets or increasing the revenue from existing customers.

The task to find a business opportunity requires a high-level analysis of procedures and processes. Efficiency and effectiveness are directly impacted by the way processes are performed. Assess these processes by considering turnaround time, error rate, and decision delays.

Identifying increases in revenue typically requires a marketing study or marketing analysis. The Farmer appreciates a high-level review of the total market, broken into key market segments. Opportunities for increased revenue through new products/services, or expansion into new customer segments are the two most common ways for demonstrating revenue opportunity.

Note: once an opportunity is identified, Business Scientists are exceptional at creating plans to fulfill the vision.

Considerations: Farmers typically have an intuitive sense of whether an envisioned effort has a reasonable chance of success. Farmers fundamentally look for revenue increase or cost reduction. Some business opportunities have both components. This task begins to identify opportunities for improvement—whether the opportunities are revenue or cost reduction. This task might identify out-of-date activities, or processes better enabled through technology.

Who understands the current processes? Who might have ideas about process improvements? Why do some processes seem to be so deeply entrenched, and others are flexible and not well documented? Who understands the current customer base and trends in the market? Why are the trends taking place?

Practices:
- Identify subject matter experts and conduct a facilitated discussion.
- Identify (5-20) primary processes performed by the group, department, or role.
- Create and use a brainstorming tool to accompany this task.
- Identify a few high potential opportunity areas related to a cost reduction.
- Identify a few high potential opportunities for improved market penetration or increased revenue.
- Classify and prioritize data into a few common themes.
- Draft a synopsis of the results.
- Provide copies to management and focus group participants and isolate the top ideas for continued work.

Promote the Project

Overview: Advertising the project informs stakeholders of upcoming change. This task decides what phase (time) of the project will be appropriate to introduce the project to the stakeholders. Advertising the project may also create anticipation or generate stakeholder interest.

Considerations: Promotion of an upcoming project can be creative or simple. Choose the form of advertising to fit the needs, budget, and project. Advertisement should be thoughtfully timed and it sets the tone for future communication. Advertising's aim here is to introduce an idea and establish appropriate expectations. Expect the advertising to *provoke* reaction, both positive and negative. This task is coordinated with and becomes part of the communication plan. Who needs to know about the initiative? Why would this group care, or be interested?

Practices:

- Note to Farmers and Scientists—advertising and promoting a project are important. Still, advertising is only part of the important communication that must take place.
- Avoid the mistaken assumption that advertising (telling about the initiative) is sufficient for the needed communication.
- Use normal existing communication for this task when possible.
- Select the best way to effectively reach stakeholders.
- Use multiple channels such as email, voice mail, and through management structures, if necessary.
- Consider the expectations that advertising will create and make sure that the form of advertising chosen meets those expectations.
- Gain management approval of the advertising method chosen and the content to distribute.
- Secure an executive sponsor or other business leader to make the initial announcement.
- Limit the initial announcements to groups who might care about the subject.
- Advertise the opportunity to the appropriate groups.
- Collect, process, and respond to feedback.

❧

Opportunity Summarized

Opportunity is the number one business priority from the Farmer's point of view. To a Farmer, it is imperative to understand the opportunity, to have an achievable vision, and for the right team to be assembled. Without confidence in these, to a Farmer, there is no opportunity and there would be little reason to invest any additional energy toward a particular effort.

To a Farmer, a clear vision statement serves as the starting point for further work. Opportunities for business improvements, especially those including metric-driven concepts such as turnaround time, error rate, and decision delays are meaningful to the Farmer. An effective way to communicate opportunities to a Farmer is by summarizing them in general categories or themes.

Concurrent with an understanding of the opportunity, the Farmer will also seek an understanding of the obligation. (Obligation is outlined in the next section). Once the opportunity and obligation are understood, an initial announcement about the opportunity becomes appropriate.

Together, the Farmer, Scientist and Artist initially convey the business opportunity to their organization by advertising it through normal communication channels. The advertising should be commensurate with the opportunities identified. Now having confidence in a compelling vision, with the identified opportunity communicated to the organization, the Farmer is ready to move forward.

Obligation

A second area of interest for the businessman or businesswoman in the role of the Farmer is obligation.

In any initiative, the Farmer asks, "What is our obligation?" Obligations do not have to be performed in contractual terms to be "binding" to the organization. Plain old keeping your promise to a customer or another business outside of a legal contract can easily be seen as an obligation, which the Farmer wants to keep. Certainly, keeping monetary obligations and contractual obligations come first. But, also, the little informal obligations, which cannot legally be enforced, are nonetheless the kind of obligations on which an organization's good name and reputation is built, itself a valuable and conveyable asset.

The Farmer is reluctant to invest time, effort, energy, and money in an effort in which the organization's obligation is not clear. A cost/benefit analysis must be performed. What is the specific cost to achieve what specific benefit? Nothing too vague or general will do in making a cost/benefit analysis. When the cost outweighs the benefit, the Farmer does not go forward and instead looks for another route. Benefits can be tangible or intangible. Actions can directly or indirectly lead to increased profit. The routes that lead indirectly to profit are the ones in greatest need to be scrutinized.

Sometimes projects appear to have some benefit, but after creating an opportunity assessment and looking under the hood, the Farmer sees that those projects that looked good at first are no longer attractive. He or she has to know when to give up a project to satisfy a business obligation in another manner.

Story: Assessing the Obligation

A Fortune 500 corporation believed its Information Technology (IT) cost to be too high. With operations in Europe, Australia and the United States, executives believed the on-going maintenance cost of computer applications might be less expensive if managed in Centers of Excellence (COE). In particular, the Australia organization had deep skills with the customer relationship management (CRM) system. If all application maintenance for the CRM transferred to the Australian subsidiary, on-going cost would be lower due partially to a lower wage rate, and partially because of easier access to the needed skills.

The opportunity was clear. The company as a whole could lower the on-going maintenance cost of an expensive application. The second half of the decision was not so clear. Off-shoring work to its own subsidiary would require time, effort, and money. Also important to the decision was the long-term obligation or commitment that would be required toward the CRM vendor. Making this decision would have effectively locked-in the organization to a long-term commitment to a CRM that some executives felt was inadequate. In this case, the obligation exceeded the opportunity and the organization opted to not take the action.

Here is an outline of two things the Farmer does to discover business obligations. Each is discussed within a framework of overview, considerations, and practices:

- List Cost and Benefit
- Quantify Cost and Benefit

List Cost and Benefit

Overview: Cost (or risk) and benefit associated with the business opportunity are itemized. Risks are grouped in categories (e.g., customer service risks, employee motivation risks, and procedural risks). Benefits are shown as hard benefit and soft benefit. Results of this task are useful in identifying potential interventions and to pre-empt issues identified.

Considerations: This task requires a hard look at the implications of the change. How might these types of changes be resisted? How might the initiative fail? Remember to examine the effect of the initiative on customers and suppliers (both internal and external to the organization). Who are the best people to participate in discovering the possible issues? Is there someone from another department or group who is adept at estimating cost? Who has credibility with executive management when estimated benefits are calculated? Is there someone on the existing team with previous experience with a similar project? Is this an opportunity to bring on a temporary team member, from outside the core group, to help with this task?

Practices:
- Form a group. Get representation from several disciplines (e.g., systems development, training, and other functions).

- Conduct focus group session. Identify implications of success (and failure) during the process of moving toward the vision.
- Rank and categorize the risks identified.
- Group benefits into two categories: Hard-savings (reduced cost, increased revenue) and soft dollars.
- Prepare a summary of the risks and benefits of the vision for review by management.
- Distribute the summary list to all participants.
- (Suggestion): Include a word of appreciation for each person's contribution.

Quantify Cost and Benefit

Overview: The process of quantifying cost and benefit is more complex than simply listing them. Validation of assumptions, separation of real benefit from soft benefit becomes even more important than in the previous task.

A common mistake is to "double-dip" the benefits with other concurrent initiatives. Ideally, each cost and each benefit have an associated level of confidence related to them.

Reduced workload (efficiency) is the most commonly misused benefit justification. Except in instances with rapid growth, efficiencies gained and illustrated as a hard benefit are misleading. Unless there is a clear commitment to reduce headcount because of gained efficiencies, then it is likely not a hard-benefit.

To illustrate the difference between a hard and soft benefit, the examples below pertain to benefits an individual might personally realize.

Examples of hard benefits include: getting a raise or reducing the overall electric bill at your home. These clearly increase income and decrease cost.

Examples of soft benefits include: gaining more personal time to organize a compact disk collection, or having the option of receiving a traditional paper bill or an electronic utility bill. These are nice to have, but do not directly impact household income or cost.

Considerations: Look for ways to quantify top-line increases in revenue, increased margin, eliminated waste (of material), reduced contract liabilities through re-negotiation, and reduced head-count. For cost, include the additional time, effort, and money required to ramp-up the new processes. Which group handles the most costly part of the process? What groups might impact the cost, but they are only indirectly part of the process? From a customer's perspective, what is the most valuable part of the process?

Practices:

- Use more than one method of estimating cost and more than one method of estimating benefit.
- Use at least one top-down approach to make each estimate. The starting point numbers ideally begin with budgets and projections from the financial statements.
- Use at least one bottom-up approach to make each estimate. Document the assumptions made, and the relationships between the assumptions along with the confidence level in each assumption.
- Identify weaknesses in each estimating technique and recalculate those using bands-of-probability (high, medium, and low). The bottom-up and top-down estimates will only rarely come out within a reasonable range on the first attempt.
- Identify a third method of estimating the values. If possible, use data from outside the organization, available in the public domain, or from a third-party vendor.
- Rationalize the three estimates—rounding the values to one or two decimal points. The best way to present this information to a Business Farmer is by using a range of values. Having the high-level numbers is important.
- Avoid displaying the detail or the mechanics of how a figure is derived, unless asked. Have the detail readily available, but a Business Farmer typically only wants to see that detail exists, not to test the calculations.

Obligation Summarized

Obligation, like opportunity is extremely important to the Farmer. Having the right team assembled, and having an established vision are components of the opportunity. This must be balanced with a reasonable and quantified estimate of the cost and benefit before a Farmer is prepared to move forward. Without some semblance of understanding the opportunity and the obligation there would be little reason to invest any additional energy toward a particular effort from a Farmer's viewpoint.

Farmers understand that in the early stages of an initiative, it is not reasonable to expect precision in all estimates of cost and benefit. Ranges of estimates are acceptable during the early stages of an initiative, with more specific values being calculated as the project moves along.

Identification of risks or potential risks is also recommended when communicating the opportunity and obligation. Having the assumptions readily available to support any calculations is also advisable. This said, the Farmer-role doesn't typically require a deep dive into the specific way a particular calculation is performed, but the Farmer will desire to know that the assumptions and calculations can be described, if necessary.

Benefits should be shown as hard benefit and soft benefit. This process is more complex than simply listing the benefits or calculating a total value. Separating the benefits in this way will decrease the common mistake of "double-dipping" some values.

One important point to note is that unless there is a clear commitment to reduce headcount because of gained process efficiencies, it is not proper to list these efficiencies as a hard-dollar benefit (i.e., a cost reduction). Efficiencies are good and possibly highly desirable, but they are not the same as real bottom-line cost savings.

Farmers may need to coach the Scientists and Artists about the relationship of opportunities and obligations. Scientists and Artists alike need to be keenly aware that opportunity and obligation are vitally important to the Farmer before he or she is prepared to move forward.

Objectives

A third area of interest for the businessman or businesswoman in the role of the Farmer lies in objectives.

It is important to understand the difference between opportunities, objectives, and goals. Objectives and goals are similar to opportunity, but are more specific.

An objective includes a description of what should be achieved; the conditions under which the achievements will be made; and a set of criteria that will be used to judge what's been done.

A well written goal states: who will achieve the goal, what action will be taken, what the measurable key result will be, and what the target date is for completion.

To illustrate:

Example Opportunity

We have the opportunity to expand our market share in California.

Example Objective

- With our existing staff, we will achieve increased market share in California through new client acquisition and increased sales volume during peak season, resulting in $5 million additional revenue compared to last year.

Example Goals

- Our sales team will identify and close three large accounts by the second quarter of this fiscal year in California.
- Our California operations team will increase sales volume to existing clients by 15% during peak season this year.

Here is an outline of what the Farmer does to create and clarify business objectives. Each is again discussed within a framework of overview, considerations, and practices:

- Clarify the objectives
- Create a list of project goals

Clarify the Objectives

Overview: In this task, a project's business objectives are clarified for the purpose of better communicating with management and staff.

Considerations: Whereas the vision statement serves as the starting point for communication, the business objective provides the starting point for focusing the activities. A business objective must fit within the organization's overall vision. Does the business objective apply to the entire organization? Does the objective apply more to one part of the organization than it does other parts? Will everyone recognize the objective as important? Who will be confused by the objective statement? Are there people from outside the core team that can participate in this activity? Should this activity be kept "close-to-the-vest" or should others be actively involved in the task?

Practices:

- Review the organization's vision, strategy, and prior business objectives of the business unit, group, or team.
- Identify opportunities for improvement through enhanced processes, functions, technology, or organization changes.
- Identify opportunities for increased revenue through new market penetration or increased "share-of-wallet" of existing customers.
- Identify constraints (or conditions) that exist or are perceived to exist. (For example, funds may be limited or access to key staff members may be difficult).
- Create a short list of the best opportunities then draft objectives.
- Confirm each objective includes a description of what should be achieved; the conditions under which the achievements will be made; and a set of criteria that will be used to judge what's been done.
- Gain team consensus. Publish. Distribute to business unit stakeholders.

Create a List of Project Goals

Overview: This task is required for all change initiatives. A set of goals is documented that specifically apply to the initiative. At least two and typically no more than five goals are created.

Considerations: Project goals should be clearly stated, measurable, and specific. Goals should be attainable and appropriate and should be constantly referred to for clarification and direction. Use goals to manage project expectations up front. Make sure key business personnel from all levels are included in this task. Who can review the drafted objectives to identify if they are written with clarity? Why are the goals important? Who might view the goals as encroaching on their turf? Who would benefit if the goals were achieved? Within the organization, are there any groups that would reject the goals?

Practices:

• Review the characteristics of a well-written project goal: Who will achieve the goal, what action will be taken, what the measurable key result will be, and what the target date is for completion.

- Review the project opportunity statement and any project objectives previously written.
- Brainstorm ideas for goals.
- Arrange ideas in common categories and combine related goals.
- Record goals using a bullet point approach stated as an action, e.g., "This project will increase customer service level by..."
- Reach consensus and commitment.
- Provide all persons involved with a copy of completed goals.

Objectives Summarized

Objectives and goals are more specific than stating the business opportunity. In practice an opportunity statement is frequently abbreviated and presented as a project objective or goal. While this is understandable short-hand in business presentations, it is wise to go through the effort to fully draft a corresponding set of objectives and goals for each opportunity.

This section outlines components of what ideally is included with an objective and a goal. An objective includes a description, conditions and criteria. A well written goal states who, what and when. The next section, Outcome, more completely describes the "conditions" component of an objective and the "what" component of a goal.

Outcome

A fourth area of interest for the businessman or businesswoman in the role of the Farmer is in the outcome of his or her business endeavors.

Farmers are very much interested in production, outcome and output, so it's important when dealing with executive teams to think in terms of what the end result will be. In the heartland, agricultural farmers are interested in the production of a particular field or herd. Using this as an illustration, the scope or boundaries of production include only the land enclosed by a fence. Business Farmers also need to know how far out the *fence* goes on a particular opportunity. They need to have clarity of the scope.

It is important to have clarity on how management approval will be arranged and what the scope is and what the initiative is, as well as what the initiative is not.

Story: Beyond Organizational Boundaries

Two of the largest aerospace manufacturers in the U.S. partnered on a multi-billion-dollar project for the military, but productions costs were running several million dollars over budget for each unit produced. The scope of the project was very broad reaching. It was apparent to both companies the scope of cost control was in fact beyond the organizational boundaries of the two companies. The scope eventually called for an extended supply chain assessment that included each of the two primary contracting companies, plus 24 of the largest subcontractors, as well as the military representative to identify cost reduction opportunities throughout the entire supply chain. By thinking in terms of what the end result should be, the Farmer can widen or narrow the perspective to control production.

With the aerospace example above, the scope of work went well beyond the boundaries of the two organizations. Facilitating change across organizational boundaries is more complex than making changes within the four walls of an individual company. Outside consultants can be useful in bridging gaps in these instances. Both companies (and in this instance almost thirty different organizations) must work together for a common end result—where all the organizations "win" in some way.

Story: Scope within an Individual Function

A mid-size company wanted to improve the value to its clients after the services had been provided. The Sales & Marketing function had an out-bound call center which was available to contact clients months or even years following the delivery of services. A separate department had formal responsibility for collecting customer satisfaction data. The company wanted to move forward with a "Value at Every Touch Point" initiative which would include the call center.

The Sales & Marketing organization sent an invitation to several individuals to participate in a discussion related to customer follow-up. At first glance, it appeared the Sales & Marketing function was encroaching on the responsibility area of other department. Until the scope of the discussion was more clearly defined to be limited to the call center, there was some confusion and hesitancy from leadership. Once the scope was more clearly defined and communicated, moving forward with the discussion became much easier.

It the example above, the scope of the effort did not cross organizational boundaries, but until the scope was defined as such, there was some hesitancy. At other times, scope will cross boundaries, and that should be clearly communicated as well. Suggestions for defining scope are provided below.

Here is an outline of two things the Farmer does to establish outcomes. Again, each is discussed within a framework of overview, considerations, and practices:

- Define Scope
- Get Management Approval
- Examine Business Results

Define Scope

Overview: This task defines the scope of the project objectives. The scope statement must clearly say what the project is. A description of what the project is not is also important. Assumptions are an important component of this statement. Spell out valid assumptions. Cast out invalid false assumptions. A scope statement is a description used to control and focus the project efforts. The task of defining the scope in a statement provides an essential opportunity to clarify any potential scope issues.

Emphasis on the importance of selecting valid business assumptions is warranted. Jeffrey Pfeffer, PhD, and Professor of Organizational Behavior at Stanford University, has emphasized the importance of testing business assumptions in several of his books and research publications. Untested assumptions can dramatically and erroneously steer an otherwise powerful business initiative off course.

Considerations: Well-defined projects have a higher probability of success of improving the business initiative. Several models and frameworks exist for defining scope, but one common framework is to define the scope of "people, process, and technology."

Break down each category, defining scope in terms of the subcategories.

- **People** might include: culture, capability, communication, roles/responsibility, reporting relationships, training, recognition systems, alignment, and compensation.
- **Process** might be broken down into functional areas in the organization, or the standard supply chain might be used: buy, make, move, store, and sell.
- **Technology** could be broken into mainframe hardware, communication equipment, operating systems, application programs, desktop technology.

Once the categories are identified, some categories will be useful for describing the scope and the other categories will be useful for describing aspects that are not relevant to the project—thereby out-of-scope. Clearly specifying the scope serves to communicate what a project is and is not. Who will feel like the scope is too broad and encroaching on their turf? Will executive management agree with the scope defined?

Practices:

- Identify the business process to be enhanced and the outcome to be achieved.
- Identify the customer segments to be addressed, or the suppliers that are included within the scope.
- Identify the assumptions. What resources are available? What kind of commitment is present? Identify the various levels of commitment and make prudent assessments of each.
- Define what the change is. Use the project goals. What actions are required? What will be resisted? What will be embraced?
- Define what the change is not. List confusing aspects of the project. List some things that others are expecting to happen.

- List alternative ways to accomplish the objectives. Using this list, describe what the project is not.
- Get business leader's acknowledgement and draft formal memos.

Get Management Approval

Overview: It should go without saying that management approval of the project plan is essential. More than mere approval, commitment must eventually be gained. That said, this task focuses on approval. Management approval (and eventually commitment) allows the project team to move forward with the project plan. The concept of "get management approval" is listed in this section because the Business Farmer will either be a candidate for approving the initiative, or will want to know what approval has been given.

Considerations: Consult or inform all management potentially affected by the project plan. This requires good communication and written approval of at least one executive to release funds. For small initiatives, a common pitfall is to fail to document agreement and approval for a project. This can be done by using the five "Os" listed in this section for farmer: Opportunity, Obligation, Objectives, Outcome, and Order. Draft a formal memo, or an email (at a minimum) with these five headings. Provide the sponsor with an overview of these five categories. Provide a place for the sponsor to sign-off (literally) on the initiative, or use the formal process that is in-place at the organization. Who is needed to be visible as the sponsor? Who needs to sign-off on projected costs as they are incurred?

Practices:
- Identify all management involved or affected by project.
- Use the five "Os" listed in this section (Opportunity, Obligation, Objectives, Outcome, and Order) to communicate the project to executive management.
- Conduct a meeting with management. Present project objectives, project and communication plan, cost/benefit analysis, and change tasks.
- Make adjustments as necessary.
- Offer management a final revised copy of the documents.
- Obtain formal approval to move forward.

Examine Business Results

Overview: This task summarizes business results of an effort even as changes are still being evaluated and fine-tuned after implementation. Communicating the results re-emphasizes the link between the vision and the results. This task corresponds to the end of a major phase in the project.

Considerations: Communicate both positive and negative results while supporting the change(s) currently taking place. The messages should encourage employees to initiate new change and support ongoing improvement. Who is interested in the business results? Why are these results important to know?

Practices:

- Review the communication plan, project objectives and goals.
- Update plan to include information about how the success of the change initiative is being evaluated.
- Identify significant aspects associated with the change (both positive and negative).
- Communicate to stakeholders both positive and negative results.
- Communicate to stakeholders: support for the change(s) currently taking place.

Outcome Summarized

The outcome of an effort is very much dependent on the scope of the effort in the same way an agricultural farmer's total production is related to the land area (scope) being harvested. To communicate a complete picture to a Farmer, the outcome must be related to the scope of an effort. At the beginning of an initiative, describe the state-of-being once the initiative is complete; then once the initiative is complete, evaluate the results for success.

In today's larger organizations, the existing business process and technology have become complex and frequently cross organizational boundaries. Getting management approval and consent from the organization units potentially involved is part of the process of clarifying an outcome. Another way of looking at this from a Farmer's perspective is the opportunity is what exists before the harvest season begins and the outcome is what is actually achieved once the harvest takes place within a particular field.

Order

The fifth and final area of interest for the businessman or businesswoman in the role of the Farmer is order. The word order has a dual meaning here. Order is related to the sequence of events, as in "the order of events", and also related to the act of issuing a command, as in "to place an order."

Farmers desire confidence in the sequence, or order, of planned events, along with back-up contingencies should events not go as planned. This section outlines the rudiments of contingency planning, as part of the order of events.

All participants in a PBC will be motivated by executive direction and approval. In this section "placing the order" by way of executive approval is also included.

Like their metaphorical counterpart, Business Farmers are very in tune with seasons or business cycles and the possibility that unpredictable events can happen. When things go wrong, Farmers have a back-up plan. Within their sense of order is a fundamental notion of continuity and contingency.

Many companies in their Year 2000 efforts became quite aware that if systems failed because of some glitch or bug, they needed to have contingency plans in place.

Story: Contingency Planning can have Ancillary Benefit

One of the largest oil field service providers on a global basis went through and documented their major business processes, identifying potential risk areas to reduce possible problems due to the Year 2000 "millennium bug."

In doing so, the organization identified process improvement areas and similarities within separate business units. Contingency plans were created for the most pressing parts of their business had their systems malfunctioned. But also, business streamlining and synergy across the organization became an ancillary benefit of going through the planning exercise.

Then with business disruptions caused by Year 2005's record-breaking hurricane season, broader ideas of contingency planning have been elevated.

Here is an outline of two things the Farmer does to maintain order in his or her business. Again, each is discussed within a framework of overview, considerations, and practices:

- Create a Contingency Plan
- Get Approval to Implement

Create a Contingency Plan

Overview: Contingency plans vary widely in their size, scope, appearance, and context. They might be as simple as a "Plan B" in case "Plan A" fails, or they might have a sophisticated set of if-then propositions. Some judgment is in order to not overdo the contingency plan, jeopardizing the time and effort required to complete the initiative's plan. Still, more times than not, contingency planning is inadequately performed.

Events having low probability but high consequence require thorough contingency planning. For example, if there is a fixed completion date that is not moveable, evaluation of risks (such as not having enough staff to complete the initiative) becomes imperative.

A basic framework for establishing a set of practical contingency steps is "time, cost, and scope." Brainstorming "what-ifs" around each of the three categories is a useful exercise. What-if time runs 10% longer than expected? What-if cost is 10% more than expected? What-if the project can not address all areas originally defined as in-scope?

Considerations: A matrix or grid is a convenient method of summarizing contingencies. Allow the left-hand column to list all of the "what-ifs" and scenarios. Allow the right-hand column to describe the action that should be taken if the scenario comes about. Many times, simply going through the effort to construct such a table will provide valuable insight in the design of the project plan itself. The project plan might become more detailed to mitigate some of the risks after going through this exercise. Who has experience with failed projects in the past that might shed some light on this subject?

Practices:

- Construct a two-column table labeled scenario on the left and action on the right column.
- Use time, cost, and scope as the basis for brainstorming, and identification of several what-if scenarios.

- For smaller projects, the table suggested here will suffice. For large projects, an entire document may be warranted.

Get Approval to Implement

Overview: The actual implementation of a project is more costly than the earlier stages of simply getting a project started, or conceptualizing the idea. This task further establishes management commitment. Management approval provides support for moving forward and implementing the change initiatives. This authorization extends beyond the more esoteric agreement that a particular outcome would be a "good thing." Management approval is formally communicated to the stakeholders.

Considerations: Visible and deliberate public commitment by management to implement the transition creates support from stakeholders. Use management commitment to engage the stakeholders. In addition to the sponsor, who is seen as highly credible to the major stakeholder groups? Who must be included as a sponsor and as having commitment in order to get the project moved forward? Who might be a roadblock at a later time that can be enlisted now, instead of later?

Practices:
- Work with key managers and executives in small groups or through individual discussions.
- Summarize the activity to-date, planned activity, objectives, cost, benefit, risk, and alternatives.
- Secure management agreement to formally communicate support for the change to stakeholders.
- Provide support to management and executives as necessary to facilitate communication.

Order Summarized

This section takes advantage of a dual meaning for the word "order." In this sense, order refers to the sequence of events—especially as they pertain to contingency planning. Also, the word serves as a reminder that all participants in a PBC respond best when a formal "order" is placed by executive management in a formal announcement and approval to implement.

For complex or highly risky business ventures, the specific methods behind contingency planning are beyond the scope of this book. At its most basic level, contingency planning includes imagining the possible things that could go wrong and identifying actions that can be taken to reduce the probability of these events, and to construct actions in case the events do take place.

Farmer Summarized

While employees throughout any organization, filling any function, and at any level might have a natural affinity toward the characteristics of a Farmer, there are several job titles that tend to foster the Farmer mentality more than others. Operational roles, executive positions, and business leadership functions tend to require and favor a farmer perspective.

The most basic interests of the Business Farmer are decreased cost and increased revenue. The Business Farmer, like the agricultural counterpart, attends to practical, operational matters. In the earlier examples sited, if a farmer sees a broken fence, the farmer simply assumes the fence needs to be mended. In a related examples dealing with a laboratory, the scientist's "home", a farmer might appreciate the outcome of a particular experiment but will be less interested in the details of how the experiment was conducted. To round out the illustrations, the farmer might recognize and appreciate the utility of the artist's tools found in the art studio, but would be more inclined to understand their utility rather than as instruments in artistic endeavors.

The Farmer section reviewed the role and interests of the Farmer by describing the Five-Os:
- Opportunity
- Obligation
- Objectives
- Outcome
- Order

Each of these areas were described by using the framework of overview, considerations, and practices (what, who/why, and how/when) in the language of Farmer, Artist, and Scientist, respectively.

By reviewing the Five-Os, project participants are better equipped to discuss an initiative with a Farmer, and Farmers are better able to translate their needs to Artists and Scientists by using the subsections of considerations and practices.

Artists and Scientists should take note that Farmers are most interested in the "what" of a situation, and they appreciate discussions framed as an "overview."

Farmers (executive management and business leaders in particular) should take note that the primary suggestion of this section is for those leading an effort to "get in the wheelbarrow" as described in the story of George Blondin.

The next section reviews the interests and viewpoints of a Business Scientist.

Part 5

Scientist

Being a Scientist

"All progress has resulted from people who took unpopular positions." Adlai E. Stevenson, 1954.

"Progress robs us of past delights." Sam J. Irving, Junior, 1983.

As with the Farmer, any given individual working on a business change may have an affinity toward the role of Scientist. Scientists appreciate progress. Scientists are comfortable working with details especially when the details pertain to their area of expertise. Scientists at times appreciate details in areas other than their expertise. Most disciplines create their own set of jargon—which serves to make communication efficient between those who practice that particular function. Progress is often accomplished in small discrete steps forward, with new lessons learned and incorporated into future actions. Like the Farmer, there are several job titles that tend to require those occupying the title to serve as a Scientist. A list of job titles is presented to illustrate those who are most typically acting as a Scientist on a business change.

- Business Subject Matter Expert
- Many Administrative Roles
- Manufacturing Expert
- Marketing Expert
- Business Analyst
- Project Manager
- Technologist
- Accountant
- Engineer

Scientists are most effective with the Artist and Farmer roles when they acknowledge the differences in communication methods and business perspective.

For the Farmer, useful tools include one or two page diagrams of the process being discussed, or the concept being analyzed. Farmers appreciate hearing and seeing how a particular idea fits into the larger context of a business change before diving deeper. A high level overview and introduction is extremely useful to begin conversations with Farmers. When Business Scientists meet with Business Farmers, they should lay out an agenda, even for a 30 minute discussion. The agenda should provide declarative sentences about the purpose of the meeting.

Enlisting Artists in a discussion ideally includes framing the dialogue within the context of the organization or an important market segment. Using an organization chart may, for example, be helpful in orienting an Artist. Artists will also appreciate a high level overview before launching into the details. A point of frustration between Scientists and Artists is the idea of clarifying specific tasks that need to be accomplished. Also, estimating the amount of effort required to accomplish a set of tasks can become frustrating. Artists in general are less apt to have metrics or measures readily at hand for listing off specific tasks they may be able to lead or contribute to. Be prepared to assist the Artist with ideas about clarifying specific actions and concrete results.

Business Scientists focus on the Five-Ps: Plan, Problems, Process, Prototype, Prudence

During my first career as a petrophysical scientist, I worked with dozens of very skilled scientists. We tended to be very methodical. We used the scientific approach of hypotheses techniques and best practices. We sequenced tests in steps, used equations and formulas, made assumptions, and took measurements of results.

These procedures and thought processes are similar to those a project manager or program manager on a large initiative should take. They are appropriate for deep subject matter experts in a particular discipline. They are skills men and women as Business Scientists use in making PBCs.

To achieve their goals, all scientists—whether in wet or dry disciplines—focus on methods, hypotheses, techniques, assumptions, best practices, phases, task steps, equations, and measurements. In the world of business, the project manager or a subject matter expert (SME), who is very deeply familiar with a particular domain of knowledge, pursue similar steps to arrive at a decision. SMEs include marketing experts, manufacturing experts, accounting experts, and others.

Technical Jargon

It is difficult to communicate particular expertise to those in the organization who do not share the same level of expertise. Business Scientists cannot solely "speak his or her own language" and expect a sophisticated initiative to succeed. Words selected and ideas described must be less sophisticated in some instances. Or, time must be taken to educate others in the meaning of specific words or technical jargon.

It is very easy to get caught in the rut of using technical jargon and risk losing others whose contributions to the success of the initiative is just as crucial. Project managers, business subject matter experts, technologists, engineers, and accountants: beware. Although Business Scientists must necessarily talk to each other by using distinct words and phrases and, especially, acronyms, they must with equal importance "translate" those same words and terms when talking or writing to others in separate areas of the business.

Common to all professions and jobs—law, medicine, and day laborers—a distinct vocabulary exists to make communication quick and easy. But confusion arises when the speaker of that unique idiom fails to provide a glossary or fails to clarify them during a meeting where members of other departments are represented.

This book includes over thirty acronyms that have a reasonably high degree of usage in various business situations. A glossary in the back of the book provides a convenient reference and description of these. New participants in a business change initiative may find this glossary helpful as they come up to speed.

If the Business Scientist talks or writes without defining his terms in a simple way for others to understand, others immediately and perhaps correctly assume that the speaker is hiding ignorance and confusion behind fancy, meaningless language. Granted, some things cannot be explained to everyone. Still, the most difficult ideas can often be summarized in layman's terms without being pedantic or condescending.

Story: Jargon Stifles Business Opportunity

As a young petrophysical scientist, I worked in a laboratory with a brilliant Ph.D. Once when talking to a client touring our lab, he began describing the process of a particular test (cation exchange capacity) we routinely performed. He droned on about ionic aluminum silicate hydroxide (clay) with a positive charge.

Unfortunately he failed to explain what he was talking about in the client's terms. In particular, *with* the test, more oil would be found. Without the test, some oil reserves would be under-estimated or overlooked.

Even though everything my mentor said was technically accurate and would have made an excellent textbook on the subject, the client was absolutely lost. The client really wanted to know why that test was important to his business. Regrettably, the client left uninformed and a business opportunity was lost.

Story: Technical People can Eliminate Jargon Too

A very seasoned and tenured IT Director at Raytheon has been in Information Technology for essentially his entire career. He appreciates the fundamental fact that technology is useful. But his real contribution to the business is that he is able to communicate. His ability to communicate accounts for the reason he has risen to a leadership position. His success was not easily come by and he wasn't just lucky. Throughout his career he has actively worked at attaining the ability to translate technology jargon into meaningful conversations with "Farmers" and "Artists."

Plan

The first area of interest for the businessman or businesswoman in the role of the Scientist lies in planning.

For the project manager or SME, it is important to plan. Logistics and schedules are also very important. Without putting plans in place, a business initiative will not likely yield business results.

Story: Poor Planning Wastes Time, Effort, and Money

I was assigned to assist an effort budgeted for about $30 million. The work included implementing an Enterprise Resource Planning application. The work had been underway for several months already, and a rather large number of dedicated employees were busy doing things. Upon arrival to the project as part of the team, it was apparent that while a lot of activity was taking place, very little progress was being made. Busy people were trying to do good work, but the work had been inadequately planned. We did eventually put a plan in place, but it was much more difficult to construct while work was in process, than had the plan been done well in the first place.

The in-depth subject of planning and creating a plan in business are beyond the scope of this book. The subject of planning in business spans several broad areas from strategic planning, to facility planning— from cost reform planning to marketing plans. With this, the three most common types of business plans are presented in this book. In their generic form, they represent the majority of plans that would apply to a PBC.

- Project plans should be developed for essentially all technology projects, process improvement projects, or organization change initiatives. These might be related to increases in revenue, or to decreased cost.
- Marketing plans should be developed for efforts to create new revenue opportunity, or sustain existing revenue.
- Supply chain plans should be developed for efforts involving the production of or movement of physical assets. These are usually cost reduction efforts.

Together, the project plan, marketing plan, and supply chain plan provide the basis for Scientists to document "how" and "when" particular actions need to take place.

Hundreds of publications with best practices for project planning, along with templates and other guidelines will be superior resources to this short section dedicated to the subject, for those interested. Still, it is instructive to review the basic elements of planning herein—which may be sufficient for less complex initiatives, even as written.

The Project Management Institute (PMI) provides authoritative and widely recognized certification for project managers.

Marketing publications far deeper in substance and scope than this book are also easily available. The basic outline of a reasonable marketing plan is provided below for less sophisticated efforts, and as a starting point for discussions on the subject.

Several certification programs exist within the marketing function. The American Marketing Association (AMA), one of the largest professional associations for marketers, has 38,000 members worldwide in every area of marketing. The Association of International Product Marketing Managers (AIPMM) provides certification for marketing product managers. Sales & Marketing Executives International (SMEI) is another alternative for identifying deeper knowledge about marketing.

Like project planning and marketing planning, there are many excellent resources for supply chain management and logistics practices. Charles C. Poirier, and separately, Donald J. Bowersox are two of the more prolific authors and authorities on these subjects. APICS promotes itself as the global leader of information and services in production and inventory management for its members.

This Scientist section provides only a rudimentary outline necessary to create one of the three basic plans common to a PBC. As with our discussion in the metaphorical role of the Farmer, each is discussed within a framework of overview, considerations, and practices:

- Make a Project Plan
- Make a Marketing Plan
- Make a Supply Chain/Logistics Plan

Make a Project Plan

Overview: A project plan includes a description of the business initiative and a list of tasks required to achieve the initiative, from beginning to end. Skills required for the initiative and the people who have the necessary skills need to be precisely identified. Stakeholders for the change initiative need to be identified and described. A project plan must include an estimate of the effort and time needed to implement the change initiative.

Considerations: A project plan should include potential areas of risk to be addressed early in the change process. The estimated timeline may be broken down into phases to enable better management of each phase. Variations from the timeline should be reported and discussed as they occur. Success factors should be included so management can determine the urgency of change initiatives. Who can be enlisted to critique the plan? What groups and individuals are likely required to carry the plan out? Are any outside resources required to assist in putting the plan into action? Will any of the team be traveling and require laptop configuration (for example)?

Practices:
- Draft components of the plan, commensurate with the complexity of the initiative to be performed:
- Write a project charter
- Develop a business case/project proposal
- Draft a budget
- Create a change management plan
- Create a communication plan
- Develop a risk management plan
- Identify procurement management alternatives
- Create a work breakdown structure by breaking the project down into phases, major activities, and tasks.
- Estimate the effort in terms of full-time-equivalent (FTE) hours.
- Use a top-down estimating technique, along with a bottom-up technique. A third method of verifying the amount of time required to accomplish the project is highly recommended.
- Establish relationships between the tasks. Find dependencies such as tasks that must start at the same time, complete at the same time, or where one task must begin before the second task begins.
- Assign skills to each task, noting that some tasks may require several people and several skills to complete.
- Identify individuals with the appropriate skills to assign to the various tasks.
- Using an automated project planning tool, allow the plan to

calculate the project "critical path" and length of time required to accomplish the initiative.

- Adjust the plan by adding or removing resources (people) from the plan, adjusting dependencies, and other features allowed by the automated tool.
- Once the plan appears complete, clearly establish what people or group of people will assume ownership of the change initiative.
- Note: Most experienced project managers add from 10% to 30% contingency to their project plan estimates. For very large efforts, complex, or high-risk efforts up to 50% contingency might be called for.
- Other rules of thumb include: Add 15-20% for management and supervision. Sometimes this is called Program Management Office, or PMO. The organization change management component of a plan should typically include about the same amount of time that is allocated to the PMO.

Make a Marketing Plan

Overview: A marketing plan, at its most basic level comes down to budget allocation. For any organization there are possibly thousands of ways to spend marketing dollars and to dedicate time and effort toward marketing initiatives. A good marketing plan provides a meaningful allocation of budget to various marketing initiatives that align with the overall business opportunities.

Considerations: Where does your organization do business or where does it wish to do business? Who are the customers, and where are they located? What are your major economic advantages? What is your major differential advantage in the markets you serve? How do you currently go to market? Do you have good distributors? What are the main organizational capabilities of your firm? When should your organization participate in a marketing endeavor, and when should you not participate?

Practices:
- Draft a marketing plan document with the following sections:
- Executive summary
- Organization capabilities (strengths and weaknesses)
- Business and environment
- Market segments

- Competition summary
- Marketing alliances
- Budget
- Optionally include the additional sections:
- Organizational structure and capacity
- New product or service idea
- Sales training programs
- Operational issues
- Cross-team dependencies
- Appendices and supporting material
- Distribute and discuss drafted document with management.

Make a Supply Chain/Logistics Plan

Overview: The subject of supply chain management and logistics is most relevant to organizations dealing with physical products, rather than less tangible services. For companies producing or selling physical products, the key processes can be summarized as buy, make, move, store, and sell. While service-oriented firms also have a supply chain, for the purposes of this section, a marketing plan will be more applicable to a service firm than will the supply chain plan as described below.

Considerations: The subject of supply chain management and logistics planning is extensive. A comprehensive supply chain plan requires many participants. Who is involved with purchasing and procurement? Who understands the manufacturing processes or other assembly processes in place at the organization? Who knows where things are stored and maintained? Who arranges for transportation, travel, and related services? Which groups participate and contribute to the sales and marketing efforts of the firm?

Practices:
- Document material flow, from internal and external suppliers to and from your organization.
- Document internal and external demand and forecasting requirements for products.
- Document needs for material requirements planning (MRP).
- Document needs for capacity requirements planning (CRP).
- Document inventory management practices in the organization.
- Document procurement and supplier plans.
- Document financial and physical controls, and reporting activity processes.

- Identify weaknesses in each area documented, along with alternatives to prioritize and sequence the work.
- Draft summaries of the top recommendations, then construct a project plan for each recommendation as described in an earlier section.

Plan Summarized

The first area of interest for the businessman or businesswoman in the role of the Scientist lies in planning. Scientists are primarily interested in the "how" and "when" of a particular subject—planning answers those questions.

The full subject of planning is far beyond the scope of this book. Even so, the rudiments of the three most common plans associated with a PBC are presented in this section.

The project plan, as described here, should be created for all technology initiatives, business process improvement efforts, and organizational change projects. A marketing plan provides the pathway to increase revenue or maintain revenue in key markets. The marketing plan, as outlined in this section, provides the Scientist the basis for contributing to decision making for the organization. Last, the supply chain management plan provides many organizations with a framework to improve their core processes, streamline operations, and thereby reduce cost.

Individuals wishing to further explore the subject of business planning necessarily need to direct their attentions toward an array of books, publications, and associations dedicated to the subject. But with the outline provided herein around the subject, planning provides the foundation for the other four interest areas of a scientist—solving problems, establishing and understanding process, experimentation through prototypes, and demonstrating prudence in the various activities.

Problems

A second area of interest for the Business Scientist is in the identification of problems and the satisfaction of solving problems. The foremost aspect in this regard is to define the problem and analyze the opportunity.

Most business problems surface first as a suspicion about a problem. The problem is not well defined or well understood. It may be in the form of an idea or a concept. Parsing the concept into smaller components gives the Scientist an opportunity to analyze the different pieces and write down possible business impacts. These same findings are later useful to Farmers and Artists in their respective communication efforts.

The Business Scientist should be aware that the root problem may not be technical or process related. The core problem may be rooted in a softer, less-tangible area related to the roles assigned to individuals, the skill sets of the employees, the cultural environment of the workplace, the rewards system in-place, or more simply a problem with communication. Too frequently, a Business Scientist will, in error, imagine a solution that is more technical than necessary—skipping over the possibility of less technical solutions. Engaging a Business Artist as a sounding board is helpful in these instances.

Here is an outline of actions the Scientist does to clarify, and later solve business problems. It is discussed within a framework of overview, considerations, and practices:
- List Main Features of the Change
- Discover the Issues

List Main Features of the Change
Overview: This task produces a summary paper of the anticipated change. A text description along with supporting diagrams is created, providing impacted groups with as much information that is available. In order for participants to help isolate potential problems or issues, they first need to understand the main features of what might be changed.

Considerations: Major changes often have several stakeholder groups. Material created in this task may need to be modified or tailored to fit each target audience. Emphasis should be placed on clarity and completeness. Some useful ways to help convey information include a matrix, graphics, diagrams, bullet points, short sentences, and use of common words. This task clarifies the scope of the project in straightforward terms so all project participants can collectively understand what the project is about. Who will need to see these diagrams and provide feedback? Why are the diagrams important to convey? Who is available to make the diagrams easy to digest and understand?

Practices:
- Review project documentation: project goals, stakeholder groups, communication plan, and the overall project plan.
- Describe the change in one paragraph. (Use a one-sentence problem statement followed by one sentence explaining why it is a business issue, followed by one sentence of a potential approach to address the problem).
- Example 1: To meet the newly established sales revenue targets, we must alter the way marketing dollars are used. The current allocation process is inadequate because there isn't a consistent guideline for expense requests and there is no evaluation of return-on-investment. We need to investigate where the best ROI can be achieved and establish manageable guidelines for the future.
- Example 2: To meet the anticipated demands of our products next year using our existing production facilities, we must take action within the next five months. Our current methods, staff, and facilities will allow for a 20% increase over last year, but they can not handle the anticipated 40% increase without significant changes. We need to explore all options, including adding another shift, improving our equipment, or streamlining the current processes.
- Expand each main feature identified into a fuller description.
- Use a diagram, picture, or matrix to help clarify each feature.
- Tailor the summary to fit each of the stakeholder groups.
- Use the summary and supporting detail to discuss potential issues or problems.

Discover the Issues

Overview: This task to draws out expertise and opinions of management, supervisors, and staff. The intention is to identify possible issues with existing work processes, difficulties in the way the people in the organization interact, or issues related to technology. This task places emphasis on perceptions of participants. Results of this task provide insight that can help during the planning process (see "Plan").

Considerations: The need here is to define the problem and discover the likely core reasons the problem exists. Because all stakeholder groups might not be identified at the time of this task, the Business Scientist should use a broad cross-section of participants. Enlisting a skilled facilitator is highly advised for this task. Notably, participants are sometimes reluctant to point out problems in their areas of responsibility. Individual interviews prior to a larger facilitated group discussion are often useful in preliminary data gathering. Who can help schedule the key interviews? Who should conduct the interviews? Who should be interviewed? Why are these people important to interview? Who is the best facilitator for the group meetings?

Practices:
- Gain a general understanding of the type of change proposed.
- Arrange brief individual (or group) meetings with management and supervisors.
- Document and listen for themes of related issues.
- Correlate data (if any) from surveys.
- Draft a Change Issues Summary paper.
- Be sensitive to needs for anonymity of participants.
- Publish the paper and distribute to appropriate management.
- Adjust the draft document to reflect new findings and discoveries from management feedback.

Problems Summarized

Most business problems first surface as a suspicion about a problem. Business Scientists are particularly adept at defining, then analyzing business problems for the purpose of reducing cost (in particular). Business Scientists are also able to evaluate opportunities identified by Farmers for the purpose of market expansion and increased revenue.

Scientists begin their problem-solving quest when the problem is not well defined or well understood. It may be in the form of an idea or a concept. By parsing the concept into smaller pieces, the Scientist identifies the root cause of a problem.

This section outlined two actions a Scientist does to identify and solve problems. By first documenting the higher level feature of the problem, and then discovering the root cause, the Business Scientist is able to devise ideas to solve a business problem. The method of addressing the problems themselves is through planning and the other "Ps" listed in the Scientist section: Plan, Process, Prototype, and Prudence.

Process

A third area of interest for the businessman or businesswoman in the role of the Scientist is process. The word "process" in this sense conveys two separate, but related concepts.

The Team Process

In the first instance, the Business Scientist follows a process to achieve an end-result. This process is typically identified and documented in a plan, such as the three general plan-types listed in the earlier section. The process a Scientist follows tends to begin at a conceptual level, followed by increasingly more specific tasks that conclude with a particular output or result. When a Scientist team member speaks of a process to be followed, typically, they are referring to the sequence of activities and tasks to be performed by the project team itself.

For standardizing processes performed by a project team, especially when the project includes technology as a by-product, the Software Engineering Institute (SEI) is a good resource. SEI is a federally funded research and development center sponsored by the U.S. Department of Defense and operated by Carnegie Mellon University.

Commercial methodologies offered by the major systems integration and management consulting organizations are extremely beneficial to large efforts in particular. Having worked as both an internal and external consultant, I can attest first-hand to the benefit of using outside assistance in large efforts. For large-scale change, it is advisable to enlist the assistance of a professional consulting organization. My heritage includes Accenture, Capgemini, and CSC. While there are dozens of exceptional global management consulting organizations, below, find a brief summary of those I am most familiar with:

- Accenture is a global management consulting, technology services and outsourcing company. Their self-description refers to "a commitment to delivering innovation through deep industry and business process expertise."
- Capgemini declares itself "a global leader in consulting,

technology, outsourcing and local professional services." Capgemini includes Sogeti-Transiciel, a subsidiary business dedicated to local professional services.

- CSC declares itself as a global leader founded on "an unbroken, 45-year record of delivering business results to hundreds of commercial and government clients worldwide." Their stated mission is to put IT to work in practical, bottom-line ways.

- In addition to the large service providers, many specialized firms offer exceptional thought-leadership. One of my favorites is George Group specializing in strategies to decrease complexity in large organizations. This firm has published exceptional thought-leadership books about fast innovation, conquering complexity, and lean Six-Sigma.

The Business Process

Separate from process being *followed* by the team is the process being *evaluated* by the team. For example, a project team may be following the tasks articulated in SDLC and using those tasks to evaluate the sales process of their organization. Used in this context, "process" refers first to Systems Development Life Cycle (explained below) and then to the business process of selling.

This section addresses both the team's process (the sequence of activities and tasks followed to achieve the project team's end-result), and the business processes (those processes performed by the organizational units to be evaluated or improved).

The Business Scientist is concerned with process, detail, design, and procedures. He or she outlines procedures and processes and adds details to the change initiative throughout. Here is an outline of four things the Scientist does to address business processes. They are discussed within a framework of overview, considerations, and practices:

- Adopt a Methodology and Team Process
- Outline Business Processes
- Write Procedures and Policies
- Put in Procedures

Adopt a Methodology and Team Process

Overview: When a large consulting organization is employed to work within a client organization, typically, the consultancy brings a proprietary methodology to the table with them. Working within the consulting vendor's methodology is usually advisable. Other times, a corporate standard is in-place, and expected to be used. This section outlines some basics around methodology. This subject is vast and beyond the scope of this book, except that the idea of selecting and adopting a team process is important. Below, three examples of methods and three standards organizations are introduced:

- SDLC
- DMAIC
- ABC
- ISO (standards, not a methodology)
- ANSI (governs standards)
- NSSN (describes global standards via the web)

Systems Development Life-Cycle (SDLC) is a generic methodology, especially useful for technology initiatives, which establishes procedures, practices, guidelines, concept development, planning, requirements analysis, design, development, integration, testing, implementation, and operations of information systems. For example, the United States Justice Department has adopted a form of SDLC for its various organizations.

DMAIC (pronounced "Duh-MAY-ick") is a highly structured problem-solving method many organizations have adopted. The letters are an acronym for the five phases of a Six-Sigma improvement effort: Define-Measure-Analyze-Improve-Control.

Activity Based Costing (ABC) is an alternative accounting technique that allows an organization to determine the actual cost associated with each product and service produced by the organization without regard to the organizational structure.

ISO (International Organization for Standardization) is the world's largest developer of standards. Although ISO's principal activity is the development of technical standards, ISO standards also have some economic and social repercussions. An understanding of ISO may influence the selection of a particular analysis methodology.

Other important standards-oriented organizations include American National Standards Institute (ANSI) and National Standards Systems Network (NSSN). ANSI is a private non-profit organization that administers and coordinates the U.S. voluntary standardization system. ANSI is the official U.S. representative to the world's leading standards bodies. NSSN is a national resource for global standards which is working toward becoming the World Wide Web's most comprehensive data network on developing and approved national, foreign, regional and international standards and regulatory documents.

Considerations: Selection of a team process is important for several key reasons. One main reason for placing emphasis on this task is that the process followed will be largely dictated by the chosen methodology. Sometimes participants will not be familiar with a structured methodology, and team training will be required. Who has prior experience with a structured methodology? Why is one method possibly better than the other choices? Will any of the impacted stakeholder groups need a certain method or approach to be used? Does the consulting vendor have a preference? What kind of training is in place for the team members around a given methodology?

Practices:

Use the Systems Development Life-Cycle (SDLC) approach:

- Develop Concepts
- Plan
- Analyze Requirements
- Design
- Develop
- Integrate
- Test
- Implement
- Operate

Use the Six-Sigma approach:

- Define
- Measure
- Analyze
- Improve
- Control

Perform Activity Based Costing analysis:

- Analyze Activities
- Gather Cost
- Trace Cost to Activities
- Establish Output Measures
- Analyze Cost

Outline Business Processes

Overview: Current processes are reviewed and refined. New processes are determined where necessary. A high level outline of new procedures and processes is drafted. Processes and policies are aligned with the organization.

Considerations: Processes, procedures, and policies have a major impact on organizational effectiveness. Therefore, it is important to make sure the processes and organization work together. Use a combination of Human Resource experts, systems experts, and functional experts to help in this task.

Practices:

- Review current processes.
- Identify processes for improvement.
- Get a Subject Matter Expert to help with content of procedures.
- Identify what the final outcome of the process is.
- Identify the first and last steps associated with the process.
- List all major steps required to complete the process (assume no exceptions occur).
- List steps that have potential exceptions and their resolution.
- Document and publish the process.

Write Procedures and Policies

Overview: This task provides employees with clear instructions or documentation of procedures and processes. Employees gain specific knowledge of how to perform new or refined processes. New workflows are documented.

Considerations: Procedure documentation can create confusion. Use a standard format. Procedure writing can be quite involved. It is important to get a skilled and experienced people in procedures documentation to help with this task. Who has experience in procedure writing?

Practices:

- Confirm that all documentation will clarify new or refined processes.
- Decide on a format for how procedures will be developed.
- Set standards for how procedures will be developed.
- With SME help, gather insight on how the process will be done.
- Draft the procedure in standard format.
- Conduct a pilot test to examine how well procedures work.
- Make any necessary revisions resulting from pilot test.
- Secure management approval for publishing and distributing procedure.

Put in Procedures

Overview: This task helps the transition from an old set of procedures into a new set. Stakeholders perform the new procedures on a specified portion of their work. This is extra workload. Do not consider the new procedures live until a specified conversion date. The temporary additional workload can be frustrating and de-motivating.

Considerations: Sometimes, implementing concurrent procedures is recommended. Avoid using the "concurrent" approach when up-front training, job-aids, or other performance support techniques are available. Concurrent use of old and new procedures is a practical way to indoctrinate employees into a new way of doing things, but the double work can become tiring. Provide a lot of moral support during the transition. Continually advertise the transition date. Make every effort to make a live-switch on the date chosen.

Practices:
- Verify procedures: clear, meaningful, usable, and accessible.
- Choose a reasonable target level for duplicate work.
- Communicate reasons for dual work, time frame, and conversion date.
- Staff must understand that while new procedures are not live during the transition, it is important to thoughtfully perform the new procedures.
- Show appreciation to staff for their extra effort during the transition.
- Celebrate the conversion date. Consider a formal destruction of the old procedures in some way (e.g., tear them up, etc.).

Process Summarized

This section reviews the third area of interest for Business Scientist. The word "process" in this section is used to convey two separate, but related concepts. The process, or methodology, a team adopts for launching and eventually implementing an effort is important. Also important are the business processes that are evaluated by the team, and that are eventually altered to meet a particular business need.

The Business Scientist follows a process to achieve an end-result. This is not unlike "the scientific method" that might be followed in a laboratory. This process is typically identified and documented in a plan. When a Scientist team member speaks of a process to be followed, typically, they are referring to the sequence of activities and tasks to be performed by the project team itself.

Three methodologies were summarized that in various situations are appropriate for a team to adopt as its standard. These methods are the Systems Development Life-Cycle, Six-Sigma, and Activity Based Costing. Other sources of insight in this area include The Carnegie Mellon® Software Engineering Institute (SEI) and the International Organization for Standardization (ISO).

Also reviewed in this section is act of evaluating the organization's business processes. Process is a significant area of interest to the Business Scientist. Process is integral to the Scientist's point-of-view and is interwoven with the remaining four Ps of the Scientist's perspective: Plan, Problems, Prototype, and Prudence.

Prototype

The creation and testing of a prototype is analogous to the experimentation and scientific discovery techniques used by a physical scientist in the laboratory. Prototypes in the business sense are frequently created and tested in a "lab" environment—a physical space set aside for the Business Scientist to test variations on an idea. So, this fourth area of interest for the Business Scientist lies in making and evaluating a prototype.

Story: Begin with Simple — Progress to Complex

Prototyping is highly recommended especially for change that is difficult to touch and feel. A Fortune 500 oil company used an increasingly more complex prototyping method to roll out new technology to all of its field operations. It started with a simple prototype in one office allowing selected employees to gain experience with the technology. As that prototype was tested and improved, it was rolled out into some slightly more complex systems. By increasing and triaging the complexity of their production facilities—starting from the least complex going to the most complex—it was rolled out as a new and highly effective technology within a period of 18 months.

Here is an outline of three things the Scientist does with regard to a prototype. Again, they are discussed within a framework of overview, considerations, and practices:

- Make a Prototype
- Try Out the Prototype
- Advertise Test Results

Make a Prototype

Overview: This task may represent considerable effort. The intent of prototyping is to identify issues and flaws. The components made during this task are working models. Give attention to the main purpose of the change.

A prototype may be created for a new business concept or service, a computer application, new instructional or educational material, a new manufacturing process sequence, or a physical product.

In both marketing and engineering, increasingly, technology that can simulate the look and design of a physical object is becoming more popular. For example, Stanford School of Business has conducted marketing tests comparing the viability of using virtual prototypes to conventional market research methods. MIT's Sloan School of Management has conducted and published similar studies.

The most common form of prototypes in most businesses today come from the Information Technology (IT) departments in the form of prototype end-user applications, from marketing departments in the form of marketing concepts, new products or brand imagery, and from engineering teams working toward creation of a new product design. Beyond IT, Marketing and Engineering, almost any other function in an organization might find a use for developing and testing a prototype. According to Merriam-Webster, a prototype is "an original model on which something is patterned." Using this definition, a prototype might even include a spreadsheet with a set of mathematical models that can be tested.

Considerations: Select components carefully. Make examples of major deliverables. Deliverables are usually tangible (can be seen, heard, or touched). Some examples are in final form. Others are a draft. All examples function and convey meaning. A broad prototype represents the entire change (in draft). A deep prototype represents one aspect only (in detail). Balance the breadth and depth of the prototype. Who is prototype developed for? Who has experience with building a prototype similar to the one being envisioned? Who should be involved with testing the prototype? How many variations of the prototype are appropriate?

Practices:
- Identify the breadth and depth of the prototype. Review the considerations listed with this task.
- Examine design documentation associated with the change.
- Make a work plan when requiring more than 10 full-time equivalent workdays.
- Get representation from stakeholder groups. Let them critique the examples throughout the development process.
- Develop each component of the prototype to the appropriate level of detail.
- Document major differences or gaps between the prototype developed and the end-product or end-result likely to be developed at a later stage.

Try Out the Prototype

Overview: A well laid-out test sequence is important. Evaluate test results. Standardized documentation provides an efficient and effective way to communicate issues and weaknesses.

Considerations: Selection of the test team is an important consideration. The team should understand the intention of the test. The objective is to identify and report errors, issues, concerns, and problems. They should expect to find problems. Their findings must be sufficiently documented. The development team must understand the nature and extent of each issue. Clear communication is the primary consideration in this task. Are all the primary stakeholder groups represented and participating in the prototype test? If not, why not? Are there any people that need to be informed about the test that are not directly part of the test? Who will be interested in the outcome of the test?

Practices:

- Confirm the availability of the test team.
- For large changes, conduct a project orientation session.
- Familiarize the testers with the objective of the trial to find problems. Clarify that big problems will be fixed and that all problems will be evaluated.
- Emphasize fixes of some smaller problems may be deferred to a later time.
- Provide testers with adequate instructions and directions to understand the nature of their task.
- Identify what is to be tested and the test criteria.
- Arrange the testing sequence in a logical way.
- Standardize the feedback by providing standard reporting forms.
- Collect feedback, monitor status, and provide support throughout.

Advertise Test Results

Overview: This task provides an opportunity for the project team to recognize the efforts of participating testers. Also, the task conveys the status of the project to stakeholder groups and management.

Considerations: Straight-talk is important. Some issues identified through the testing process may not be addressed in the ultimate rollout. Describe reasons why issues deemed significant are not being addressed. When done well, this task builds confidence among the stakeholder groups. Who will want to know about the test results? To what level of detail should the test results be revealed? Why will the various groups be interested in the test results? Are there any concerns that are directly addressed by the test results? Will any groups have new questions that come out of the testing process?

Practices:

- Note to Farmers and Scientists—advertising and promoting a project are important. Still, advertising is only part of the important communication that must take place. Do not mistake advertising as a substitute for communication planning.
- Review the overall communication strategy. Review results from the prototype testing.
- Determine the most appropriate way to communicate test results. For large changes, more than one media type may be appropriate.
- Craft the messages tactfully, graciously, and honestly. Consider the following outline as a starting point (for a report): (1) Overview of change project (2) Prototype test overview (3) General outcome of test (4) The next step (5) Acknowledgments and thank you.
- Enlist others to review the memo or report for content and grammar.
- Publish and distribute the report, memo, or other communication.

❧

Prototype Summarized

Like the other areas of interest to the Scientist, the subject of Prototype is vast and varied. This section introduced the concept that a business prototype is similar to the tests used by a physical scientist in the laboratory. In fact, prototypes in the business sense are frequently created and tested in a "lab" environment.

Drawing from Merriam-Webster's definition that a prototype is "an original model on which something is patterned," we can see that almost all aspects of business can and do use prototypes to test concepts, ideas, and products.

IT departments, accountants, marketing departments, and engineering groups frequently make use of prototypes in today's businesses. Farmers and Artists alike will frequently be asked to participate in the Business Scientist's prototype endeavors. Developing, testing, and then communicating the test results are all important aspects of the prototype process. Prototypes are interwoven with the other four "Ps" of interest to a Business Scientist: Plan, Problems, Process, and Prudence.

Prudence

Merriam-Webster's online dictionary defines prudence as follows:

1. The ability to govern and discipline oneself by the use of reason.
2. Sagacity or shrewdness in the management of affairs.
3. Skill and good judgment in the use of resources.
4. Caution or circumspection as to danger or risk.

Each description correctly applies to the fifth and final area of interest for the Business Scientist.

Business Scientists fill many and varied roles in today's organization. This list includes analysts, technologists, marketing experts, project managers, accountants, engineers, manufacturing supervisors, and many roles where expertise in a given field is important.

The framework of this book generally presumes that a Business Scientist is typically responsible for implementing a business change on a day-to-day basis. A project manager in particular is usually looking at the tasks ahead, the resources available to perform the tasks, and the quality of work that is being performed. Implementation includes tracking and monitoring. The word "prudence" captures the essence of what a Business Scientist is concerned with during the implementation of a business change.

Because benchmarking, use of metrics, problem solving, and best practices are important to many Business Scientists, a suggested excellent resource for these endeavors is American Productivity & Quality Center (APQC). APQC is a research organization that solves business problems in these very areas.

Borrowing again from the definition of prudence "skill and good judgment in the use of resources", it is also appropriate to elevate the importance of enlisting the organization's accounting experts participation during a PBC. The American Institute of Certified Public Accountants (AICPA) and its predecessors has been committed to member service and the public interest, serving the accounting profession since 1887. Every organization's accounting department holds a rich set of information useful to PBC.

One additional source of highly valuable and *prudent* information is Business Research in Information and Technology (BRINT). BRINT was originally conceived to bridge the gaps between business and technology, data and knowledge, and theory and practice. It has indexed a rich set of publicly available information online for a wide variety of topics applicable to PBC.

Accounting practices, benchmarking, and other best practices are part of the prudence that is important to the Business Scientist. Here is an outline of three things the Scientist does to demonstrate prudence during a business initiative. Again, they are discussed within a framework of overview, considerations, and practices:

- Make a Scorecard
- Monitor the Change
- Provide Follow-up Support

Make a Scorecard

Overview: This provides quantifiable measures to the project team and stakeholder groups. This task helps communicate on-going results. An easy to understand measure of the change is tracked as a function of time. Depending on the complexity and importance of the PBC, a tracking scorecard might be sufficient. For some initiatives and in some organizations, a more robust "balanced scorecard" approach may be preferred.

A widely adopted approach to strategic management was developed in the early 1990's by Drs. Robert Kaplan (Harvard Business School) and David Norton. Their system is called a 'balanced scorecard' and minimizes some of the weaknesses of earlier management approaches. A balanced scorecard includes measures of financial health, customer attention, process efficiency, and people (learning and growth) management. Adopting a robust balanced scorecard approach within an organization can take up to several months. A specialty organization, The Balanced Scorecard Institute, has insights worthy of reviewing at their web site. This organization provides a central source of balanced scorecard information applicable to government, nonprofit and commercial organizations.

Considerations: Changes can seem intangible. Changes are often very difficult to quantify. Even so, it is important to have a way to measure the change. Caution should be taken not to make the measurement difficult to understand. Ideally, the presentation of the scorecard will be interesting to look at or to provide a quick synopsis without having to deeply analyze its meaning. Who needs to know about the progress being made? Who will be motivated by progress? Why is the progress important to the business? Who might be able to creatively assist in developing a concise way to track and report progress? What are the primary interests of executive management regarding this change initiative?

Practices:

- Gather potential measurement items. Review project goals, cost and benefit, change opportunities, and main features of the change.
- Select up to five items (depending on the magnitude of change) as the project Key Performance Indicators (KPIs).
- Brainstorm some creative ideas about how to track, measure, and report each of the KPI measurements.
- Make a data collection notebook or central area for maintaining measurement values as a function of time.
- Create a graphic that can be published in a prominent area. Label with a title, a brief explanation of the change; the graphic itself; an explanation of how to interpret the graphic and key dates.

Monitor the Change

Overview: This task quantifies process improvement due to specific change initiatives. Examples of improvements realized from process and procedural changes include productivity gains, efficiency improvement, levels of effectiveness, and increased quality. Perform this task to verify the level of success due to a process change.

Considerations: Each change initiative has Key Performance Indicators (KPIs). These factors are used to quantify success levels of the change. Are there convenient ways to gather the metrics that are already in-place? Who is in the best position to contribute data in an on-going manner?

Practices:

- Identify KPIs for the transition initiative. Identify overall KPIs for measuring the productivity and performance of the business processes.
- Monitor the business processes based on the KPIs as a function of time.
- Watch for trends in the data.

- Maintain a proactive watch on the data and respond before minimum threshold values are approached.

Provide Follow-up Support
Overview: This task provides support to make sure change initiative is successful. Follow-up support is flexible and is offered in many different forms. Follow-up support is offered until no longer needed. This task measures that the full potential value is being met, along with extra support where it is needed.

Considerations: Follow-up support may be needed immediately or anytime after the change initiative is implemented. Feedback from stakeholders should be continuously monitored to assess if follow-up support is needed. Who should be responsible for collecting follow-up support feedback? Who should be responsible for providing the actual support? Does this need to be communicated?

Practices:
- Gain feedback from stakeholders through interviews, observations, questionnaires, etc.
- Assess areas needing follow-up support.
- Arrange follow-up support.
- Decide how to monitor success of follow-up support.
- Provide follow-up support until no longer necessary.

Prudence Summarized
The making of a *scorecard* and then monitoring the change with provisions of follow-up support are among the actions often taken by the Business Scientist once a PBC has been largely implemented.

Drawing again from Merriam-Webster, prudence is "skill and good judgment in the use of resources." Together, the tasks described in this section provide the Business Scientist a method to administer good judgment in the use of business resources.

By using quantifiable measures, the Business Scientist and others are able to confirm productivity gains, efficiency improvement, levels of effectiveness, and increased quality. Where the improvements are less-than-expected, additional support is put into place, to make sure change initiative is fully successful.

Because the framework of this book generally presumes that a Business Scientist is often responsible for implementing a business change on a day-to-day basis (e.g., the Project Manager), this section on

Prudence appropriately resides as the last and final area of interest for this role. Prudence captures the essence of what a Business Scientist is concerned with during the implementation of a business change.

Scientist Summarized

The Business Scientist role includes many possible functions and levels within an organization. These range from marketing to engineering and from the shop-floor to executive management positions. The Business Scientist is an expert in a particular aspect of business, be that aspect related to a service or a product.

The Scientist role, similar to the Farmer attends to practical matters. But unlike the Farmer role, a Scientist becomes deeply involved with the details of a business operation. Where the Farmer is broad, the Scientist is deep. Later, we will discover that the Scientist also holds some similarity to the Business Artist—specifically in the area of inventiveness. Still the Business Scientist is set apart from the other two roles by the ability to deal with complexity in a very detailed manner.

At the beginning of the book, we read the example where if a scientist observed a broken fence, the scientist would think in terms of "how" to properly fix the fence—the materials and resources required, along with the time schedule. Planning and problem solving are key characteristics of the Business Scientist.

This section reviewed the role and interests of the Business Scientist by describing the Five-Ps:
- Plan
- Problems
- Process
- Prototype
- Prudence

Each of these areas were described by using the framework of overview, considerations, and practices (what, who/why, and how/when) in the language of Farmer, Artist, and Scientist, respectively.

By reviewing the Five-Ps, project participants are better equipped to discuss an initiative with a Scientist, and Scientists are better able to translate their needs to Artists and Farmers.

Artists and Farmers should take note that Scientists are most interested in "the how and when" of a situation, and they appreciate discussions framed as "best practices."

Scientists (e.g., project managers, technologists, marketing experts, and engineers) should take note that the primary suggestion of this section is for those providing expertise in their given area of responsibility is to *reduce the technical jargon.*

The next section reviews the role and points-of-view of a Business Artist, and the relationship of the Artist to both the Scientist and Farmer.

Part 6

Artist

Being an Artist

"Progress might have been all right once, but it is gone on too long." Ogden Nash (attributed)

"It used to be a good hotel, but that proves nothing. I used to be a good boy for that matter." Mark Twain, 1869.

As true with the Farmer and Scientist, any given individual working on a business change may have an affinity toward the role of Artist. Like the other perspectives, there are several job titles that tend to expect those occupying the title to serve as an Artist. A list of job titles is presented to illustrate those who are most typically acting as an Artist on a business change.

- Communication and Training Specialist
- Organization Development Specialist
- Some Management Consultants
- Some Marketing Disciplines
- Business Strategist
- Some Sales Roles
- Some HR roles
- Graphic Artist

Business Artists focus on the five-Cs: Culture, Communication, Creativity, Capability, and Core-HR

Artists are interested in abstractions, concepts, models, and taxonomies. Many times, PBCs made within an organization are made by consultants or internal entrepreneurs acting as Artists. Artists are visionary and creative and constantly look for imaginative but realistic ways to increase profit.

I have had the opportunity to work around people who play many different musical instruments, create paintings, dance, and practice other artistic endeavors. Focusing on musicians for the moment, they are very accomplished on certain instruments. Musicians, frequently talk in terms of abstractions and concepts, using words in one sense to convey meaning in another. For example, the *feel* of a certain rhythm, or the *brightness* of a particular tone might serve as a musical description.

Business Artists frequently approach business opportunities similar to a painter, sculptor, or composer. They act and talk artistically. Industries that are not obviously similar are compared to each other. Functions within an organization are considered as if they are separately performing instruments within the same orchestra (for example), perhaps playing in-sync with each other or not. At times, understandably, these comparisons do not resonate with the Scientists, especially. Both Farmers and Scientists tend to appreciate the more tangible and concrete forms of business.

With this, I have chosen to include the majority of "People" related topics under the Artist area of interest for several reasons. Artists, more-so than Farmers and Scientists are comfortable dealing with the wide variations and unpredictable nature of individuals, groups of employees, and the culture within large operating units and companies.

The gap between Scientists and Artists way of looking at a business opportunity is underscored by the recent emphasis Carnegie-Mellon has placed on the "People" aspect of business change through a robust set of "People" best practices can also be explored through this organization.

In particular, the People Capability Maturity Model® (P-CMM®) is a framework that helps organizations successfully address their critical people issues. Based on the best current practices in fields such as human resources, knowledge management, and organizational development, the P-CMM® guides organizations in improving their processes for managing and developing their workforces. From the web site, (as of the writing of this book), a 700+ page document with People best practices is available to download, print, and use subject to the copyright as stated.

So while the Business Artist is able to easily work within the "People" ebbs-and-flows of a business, the Artists are also able to create new ideas that often have incredible usefulness.

The very act of creativity runs counter to many of the ideas Scientists hold dear—with their desire to turn concepts into a process that can be measured, for example. And the iterative nature of being creative sometimes challenges what appears to be an obvious solution to the practical side of the Farmer. With this, it is appropriate to introduce the primary suggestion for Business Artists as they interact with their colleague Scientists and Farmers. That is, Artists should work toward speaking about concrete actions and concrete results.

Actions and Results

In business, the most successful Artists are able to first think like Farmers and Scientists. Using the language and perspective of Farmers and Scientists allows an Artist to engage others into new territory and new ideas. Without acknowledging the operational viewpoints of a Farmer and the practical viewpoints of a Scientist, the Artist may become frustrated when trying to enlist other colleagues. An Artist needs to speak in concrete terms to the Farmers and Scientists.

Often, when it comes to allocating funds during cost cutting time, the first thing to eliminate is the "Art" described in this section. The Artist needs to understand and acknowledge that their work is vitally important, but is sometimes seen as "extra" or even superfluous to the Farmer and Scientist colleagues.

Some Farmers and Scientists undervalue the role of Artist for unfortunate but understandable reasons. It is difficult to discern whether the ideas of the Artist are in fact leading to concrete decisions and adding value to the initiative or whether the Artist is simply arm waving. Artists should return to a discussion about action and concrete results when they talk to Farmers and Scientists. The Scientists will appreciate hearing things about actions that are going to be taken, and the Farmers will appreciate hearing about concrete results.

Story: Artists may be more lenient

As a mediocre guitar player I was once in the company of a dozen musicians sitting around jamming. One of them was a very gifted jazz guitarist. I was not worthy to be with them, but I sat on top of my amplifier pretending to play—many notes were purely at random. After we finished, the jazz guitarist commented how he enjoyed my playing because it was "way out there."

As a gifted artist, he may have appreciated the randomness in my limited improvisation, and he may have been encouraging me because he too at one time had lesser artistic talents. Had my playing been heard by a Farmer or Scientist as described in this book, the comments would have been less generous.

Artists in the business world are similar to those is the jazz guitar story. Some Business Artists are sufficiently gifted to just "wing-it" with ideas and new concepts — similar to a jazz guitarist doing improvisation. Both the Farmer and the Scientist will tolerate and even invite a gifted Artist to participate. The art will be appreciated, embraced, and used. New and unproven Business Artists are not so readily accepted by the Farmers and Scientists. Creativity is sometimes an iterative process. The end-result cannot be described easily because the art has not begun to be created. In most businesses today, the Farmer and the Scientist roles are relied on first when PBC is being made. Artists should not expect the Farmer or Scientist to fully embrace the *considerations* of business change. The Business Artist will be more successful when he or she communicates in the *practices* of business science and the *overviews* of business farming.

This section offers explanations to the Farmers and Scientists, so they can better understand the perspective of a Business Artist. Also, within each area, specific suggestions to the Artist are provided in how to communicate the concepts to a Business Scientist or Business Farmer. These suggestions are found as the first bullet point in the Practices.

Culture

The first area of interest for the Business Artist lies in Culture.

Culture is a frequently used word but less frequently understood. Farmers and Scientists may draw on the word, but not necessarily with a deep understanding of what it may mean.

I have had the pleasure of working with about 50 large organization clients in the U.S., Mexico, and China. Certainly, there are real cultural differences from organization to organization among nations. But even organizations with headquarters on adjacent floors in the same towering skyscraper have differences in their culture. Ignoring culture can sometimes cause business setbacks that could have been avoided if more attention had been paid to these attributes.

Cultural attitudes, assumptions, and behaviors can be observed and catalogued. But even this leaves the question about *what to do with these observations.* I have found that the concept of organization characteristics can serve as a proxy for understanding culture. Further, once the characteristics are identified, it is possible to construct new organization symbols, ceremonies, and celebrations to reinforce desirable attitudes, assumptions, and behaviors.

Merriam-Webster online dictionary defines "characteristic" as a distinguishing trait, quality, or property. In most business settings, approaching the concepts of culture through this somewhat more understandable idea of characteristics has proven useful.

Story: Address Culture to Reduce Risk

A $10 billion a year oil manufacturer, refiner, and transporter made plans to implement a robust and integrated set of business applications. The team documented the organization's cultural characteristics and then compared the results against idealized characteristics of a company that would readily accept this type of a business change. Several areas within the company culture were identified that would have threatened the success of the initiative if not addressed.

In this instance, the new business system would help the company become more operationally efficient. In particular it benefited the company's financial accounting organization. But the sales and marketing had always operated in a very customer intimate manner. The shift in becoming more operational efficiency went against the customer intimacy practiced by the sales and marketing groups. Identifying the differences early allowed the team to address risks of employee resistance earlier through good communication planning and other interventions.

A single web search for books on corporate culture will retrieve well over 1,000 recently published works on the subject. Covering the concepts and applications of cultural change are beyond the scope of this book, except to provide some highlights to instruct Artists how to communicate the importance of the subject to their colleague Scientists and Farmers. And also, Farmers and Scientists can browse this section for a cursory understanding how culture and the other four Cs relate to their respective areas of interest.

Here is an outline of four things the Artist considers in Culture. As with our discussion of focus issues in the metaphorical roles of the Farmer and Scientist, each is discussed within a framework of overview, considerations, and practices:

- Learn about the People
- Design Celebrations and Symbols
- Have a Celebration
- Respond to Organization Transition Issues

Learn About the People

Overview: This task includes analysis of the stakeholder groups likely to be impacted. Through this task, it becomes apparent that different groups have unique needs and requirements. This task identifies "people issues" and "people opportunities."

Considerations: Enlisting an expert organizational change consultant or using HR professionals to lead or substantially participate in this task is recommended. Who is familiar with the "way things are done around here" and who is possibly new to the organization that can contrast those norms against other organizations? What is the relationship between written policy and employee expectations? Are there any "unwritten rules" that employees assume to be true?

Practices:

- State to the Farmers and Scientists "This task identifies high level characteristics of each group so a plan can be created to improve future communication, training, and changes in roles."

- Draw insights from previous results of diagnostic tools and/or surveys.
- Using focus group sessions or structured interviews identify potential strengths and weaknesses of the organization's culture (or characteristics) pertaining to improved processes.
- Classify the data gathered from focus groups and interviews into a few common themes.
- Draft a synopsis of the results. Provide copies to management and focus groups. Indicate how the information might be used to improve business results.

Design Celebrations and Symbols

Overview: This task identifies desired behavioral norms. It develops rituals, symbols, and ceremonies to support and maintain the new culture in which businesses find they need to operate. Most change requires some cultural modification to support it.

Considerations: Corporate culture is recognized by its symbols, celebrations, and ceremonies. Deliberate use of business unit rituals, symbols, and group celebrations and ceremonies will reinforce a particular set of attitudes, assumptions, and beliefs. Common examples include celebrating birthdays, introducing new employees to everyone, arranging Friday afternoon get-togethers, holding company picnics, and sending letters of congratulation. A more substantial example may include the use of bonuses and the manner bonuses are administered. Who has led a recent motivating event? Why might some celebrations be frowned upon? Is there an opportunity to introduce a new kind of celebration into the organization to emphasize a new change?

Practices:

- State to the Farmers and Scientists "This task identifies cost-appropriate ways for each team to celebrate their success, so that standards and guidelines can be established and communicated up-front rather than after-the-fact."
- Identify needs of employees, e.g. behavioral norms. Look at existing rituals, symbols, and ceremonies and use all that apply.
- Design new rituals, symbols, and ceremonies to aid in meeting employee needs and business objectives.
- Obtain opinions and feedback from employees.
- Obtain management approval for cultural change actions.

Have a Celebration

Overview: This task encourages formal planning for change initiative celebrations. Celebrations are important. The celebration itself is designed to reinforce positive aspects of the change. It is an opportunity to publicly commend people who have actively helped bring about success. It takes on many forms. Creativity and good planning make this task a significant part of the overall initiative.

Considerations: Plan. Be creative. Be appropriate. Be professional. Be fun. Be interesting. Be fair. A celebration does not have to be a big blowout, but it should be commensurate with the magnitude of the change. Celebrations tend to set a precedent for future expectations. There is potential risk in both under-doing and over-doing a celebration.

This is a great opportunity to enlist a broader group of participants. Who might be great at leading and coordinating this event?

Practices:

- State to the Farmers and Scientists "This task includes monitoring that team leaders comply with the standards previously established for celebrations."
- Plan and get ideas for this task well in advance. Confirm a budget.
- Get some creative ideas on the table. A celebration might not be a single event; it might last throughout the week; it might resemble a party or something entirely different.
- Confirm that everyone involved with the change has an opportunity to participate in the celebration.
- Use the change initiative name in the celebration theme or incorporate some aspect of the change into the celebration itself.
- Include stakeholder participants in planning and coordinating the event.
- Recognize significant and special contributors to the change.

Respond to Organization Transition Issues

Overview: Information gathered in certain areas of operation in the organization will determine if any action is necessary to address organizational issues. Develop a list of possible actions to take.

Considerations: Observe the environment after a transition effort has been implemented. Ask questions such as "Is the organizational structure working?" Small adjustments to the organization design may be appropriate. Is there someone in the impacted stakeholder group who can shed light on how well the transition has worked? What lessons learned can be applied to other groups that haven't yet been impacted?

Practices:

- State to the Farmers and Scientists "This task suggests small adjustments to distribution of work across the impacted organization."
- Observe the environment of business units after transition has been implemented. Look for effectiveness of leadership, effectiveness of communication, and organizational restraints that cause confusion.
- Determine if action is warranted to adjust organizational structure.
- List possible actions.
- Provide management with the results of this task, even if no further action is required.

Culture Summarized

With well over a thousand recently published books dealing with the subject of corporate culture, cultural change, and similar variations of the topic culture, this book can not reasonably cover the breadth of the topic in one section. That said, the idea that culture impacts the success or failure of a business change initiative is hard to ignore.

Business Artists, more so than their Farmer and Scientist colleagues, are able to work within the sometimes elastic and changing nature of organizational culture. Some Artists may only be able to "understand" or "feel" the culture—and they may not be well equipped to articulate exactly "what the culture is." Still, the Artists ability to discern when something "feels" right or wrong is an important data point to draw from.

Culture can be defined as being the set of attitudes, assumptions, and behaviors of a group of individuals. Culture can be observed and recognized through that same group's symbols, rituals, and ceremonies. Some business change efforts require little-to-no attention toward the culture, because the change is consistent with who and what the organization "is". In other circumstances, an initiative introduces something new that is contrary to the *way things have been* and employee attitudes, assumptions, and behaviors do need to be taken into account.

Great communication, attention toward building the right kind of capability through training and education, and other core Human Resources initiatives are the most direct way to reduce business risks associated with culture change or "people" issues. The Business Artist is well equipped to help with these things, along with their affinity toward creativity—each of which are explored below.

Communication

A second area of interest for the Business Artist is communication. Where the Farmer *sees* the big picture, the Business Artist is able to *communicate* the big picture. Importantly, the Artist communicates detail in an approachable and understandable manner.

Story: Communication without Action Doesn't Work

Sadly, there are stories about communicating poorly. In this instance, the communication was simply not true.

A mid-size firm Tennessee experienced a thirty percent turnover rate per year. Consequently, there was a lot of retraining and a lot of new hiring going on, and the turn in the workforce itself was costing a lot of money. The profit margin suffered. The senior leadership team had started to use words and phrases like "empowerment" and "high-powered work teams" in their communication.

The problems persisted, so they brought in consultancy to reengineer the shop floor and put in a new manufacturing resource planning system, a MRP system, to increase production. But the root issue was not faulty technology or processes, rather executive management's words and actions were not in line with each other.

The truth in the situation was that the organization paid employees better than other similar jobs in that area of the state, and management was very command-and-control oriented. Management expected their well-paid employees to simply do as they were told—management didn't really mean the words like "empowerment."

Communication, of course, needs to happen. It's not a luxury but an essential. Many Farmers and Scientists equate the role of the Artist in business as one who communicates to achieve organization change. To that extent, the Artist must communicate what a project initiative is—as well as what it is not. A good Artist will anticipate and clarify confusing information so that Farmers and Scientists can rule out preconceptions to arrive at a correct understanding.

There are some marked differences between types of communication effort, so let's take a look at these.

Change enabling communication. Communication for invoking change should be very stakeholder-centric. It should be scoped to target only the groups that are impacted by the change. This is the type of communication which is vital to a PBC.

Project-team communication. The project management team should be responsible for its communication within the project team itself. Too frequently, a Business Artist (communication specialist) is assigned this role. This is rarely the best use of a communication specialist's talent.

Corporate communication. Communication about change does not and should not be equated to revamping corporate communication processes. Ideally, change enabling communication can operate within the existing processes of an organization.

Public Relations (PR) communication. Internal communication about business change should be explicitly differentiated from public relations type of communication. The PBC communication leader needs to work with PR at times. Still, PR is external to the organization and a PBC deserves clear attention to the internal stakeholder groups.

The Business Artist, who is assigned to a PBC as a communication specialist will frequently be tagged for all these varieties of communication. My suggestion is to clearly separate these different communication efforts. While each of these communication types is important, only the first two categories are emphasized in this book. Solid *change enabling communication* is required for a successful PBC (managed by a Business Artist), whereas project team communication is usually best managed by the project manager (often a Business Scientist).

Here is an outline of how the Artist communicates. As with our previous discussions, each is discussed within a framework of overview, considerations, and practices:

- Identify the Stakeholders
- Make a Communication Plan
- Give the Project a Name
- Keep Up the Communication

Identify the Stakeholders

Overview: All groups of people affected by the change initiative are identified and described. Skills and ability may be assessed. The culture might be evaluated and documented.

Considerations: Prior training and experience of stakeholders should be considered. The stakeholder reaction to any change initiative determines the success of the project. Who will be concerned or interested?

Practices:

- State to the Farmers and Scientists "This task identifies the specific communication needs and possible business concerns of the impacted groups related to the project."
- Identify all persons affected by the change initiative.
- Make a list of stakeholders.
- Organize names in a spreadsheet or similar tool with contact information such as phone number, office location, and email address.
- Identify skills or other pertinent information related to each stakeholder group.
- Brainstorm why each stakeholder group should be interested in the change—and why there might be hesitancy among the group for becoming engaged with the change.
- Determine prior training and experience of stakeholders to the degree this is important to the change.
- Determine other obstacles related to each group that might get in the way of communicating with the group, or prevent collecting feedback from the group.

Make a Communication Plan

Overview: This communication plan is not intended to facilitate communication within a project team itself. Neither is this task intended to pre-empt an organization's corporate communication process or corporate communication organization. Rather, this task is intended to create a plan to engage the staff who will be impacted by re-organized functions, new technology, or improved processes. To the extent possible, this communication plan should be created to work within the corporate communications organization methods, and coordinated with the project team communication.

Considerations: Clearly explain the intentions and planned end-results of the effort to the stakeholders. The way messages are communicated plays a large part in employee attitudes about change and will influence involvement and commitment. In this instance, active use of the technology by business unit leaders, high-touch demonstrations, and thoughtfully delivered training should be considered as part of the overall communication plan. Has Corporate Communications been informed about the change, and has that organization been consulted about the best ways to communicate? Are there any team members who are particularly adept at communicating? Who might be helpful in developing slide-show presentations, or drafting emails to be distributed?

Practices:

- State to the Farmers and Scientists "This task creates a plan for communication to be distributed, then for feedback to be evaluated."
- Identify all stakeholder groups. Note that some people will be part of more then one group. All impacted staff will be part of at least one group.
- For each group, document: preferred media types, influential communicators, key messages, and potential areas of concern or misunderstandings.
- Create spreadsheet. Each row represents a communication event.
- Include these column headings on the spreadsheet: (1) Communication Event Identifier (2) Stakeholder Group Name (3) Media to be used (4) Message summary (5) Sender of the communication (6) Method for Gathering Feedback (7) Timing of the communication event
- Complete the spreadsheet by summarizing each planned communication event on one row in the spreadsheet, with information filled out under each of the seven column headings listed above.
- Include a process for quality assurance and feedback monitoring
- Plan to use front-line supervisors for delivering the most provocative messages to the organization. Reach the front-line supervisors through direct interaction with the executive team, educating them about the planned change, reasons for the change, and process for change.

Give the Project a Name

Overview: This task is an important component of project communication. A change initiative name helps uniquely identify a change effort. While on the surface this task may seem trivial, a well-formed initiative name has considerable value. A poorly formed name can have a negative effect.

Considerations: An ideal project name is brief, descriptive, easy to remember, likable, interesting, and meaningful. Use this opportunity to get other people involved. Be creative. Ask for suggestions from the stakeholder group. Consider having a contest. Use a name that sounds like a sequel of a previously successful change: Successful Change II. Create a meaningful acronym that makes a word. Can this process be used as a way to promote or introduce the coming change? Are there some key people who should contribute to this activity? Who are some creative employees, possibly outside of the department, that can help with this activity? Some ideas or names might be trademarked or in some other way not fitting with corporate standards. Is there someone from the marketing department responsible for branding that should be involved, at least on a consulting basis?

Practices:

- State to the Farmers and Scientists "This task is important to create efficiency during the project itself. Having a clear project name will streamline project communication."
- Evaluate the relative importance of this task. High profile, substantial, or difficult changes require thoughtful attention to this task.
- Choose approach to finding name; e.g., assign a small group to come up with possibilities; have a team lunch or naming party.
- Select three or four candidate names. Evaluate the names using the following guidelines: brief, descriptive, easy to remember, and meaningful. A visual image, icon, or graphic can enhance a name.
- Avoid infringement of register trademarks and explore the possible value of registering the selected name.
- Avoid using the organization logo or brand name with the project name. Usually there are corporate standards about the proper use of a company logo and brand. This is a common mistake that many well-intended teams encounter.
- Select one of the names. Get a consensus. Publish the result to participants.

Keep up the Communication

Overview: Communication remains a significant part of successful change. This task ensures communication efforts are continued even after the change has been implemented. Collecting feedback from stakeholder groups is an important part of this task.

Considerations: Provisions must be made to allow the Project Team to respond to issues unearthed in this task. Not all issues have to be immediately addressed. However, all issues must be fixed, explained to satisfaction, or guaranteed to be addressed by some future time. Who is best equipped to quickly get answers compiled for questions that arise?

Practices:

- State to the Farmers and Scientists "This task is an update to the original communication plan based on new information that will be analyzed."
- Define and clarify the extent to which the Project Team has the authority to respond to potential issues.
- Use informal data gathering techniques to document the general attitudes and feelings of the stakeholder groups.
- Design and use more formal data gathering devices such as a project suggestion box, a project bulletin board.
- Compile direct and indirect information. Format the information to be distributed to the stakeholder groups.
- Create a response to each issue. Include some good news and facts/figures to include with the response. Publish issues and responses.
- Consider using creative ways to communicate project success, statistics, progress, and status. Provide timely updates to the information.

❧

Communication Summarized

This topic, like the topic of corporate culture, has hundreds of recent books published that explore the various nuances of great communication. This book intends only to elevate the importance of communication during a PBC—and that change enabling communication is distinctively different from on-going corporate communication or project team communication. In particular, the concept of stakeholder feedback is imperative to communication during business change.

This section outlines the importance of clearly identifying the impacted stakeholder groups, the general process of constructing a communication plan, the advantages of giving a project a name, and finally the importance of continuing communication throughout the change initiative.

To the extent possible, change enabling communication should be conducted in unison with other corporate communication requirements. In all instances, change communication should comply with corporate standards in the use and/or modifications of the organization logo or brand.

Communication is both a science and an art. Communication is listed within the Business Artist section because of the close relationship of communication best practices, organization culture, and the creativity that can go into a communication effort.

Creativity

A third area of interest for the businessman or businesswoman in the role of the Artist is creativity. This section is focused on the activities a Business Artist may perform to "draw-out" the creativity from the organization, rather than "be creative" as an individual or as a group.

Per Merriam-Webster online dictionary, the word "create" means "to bring into existence." In business, we create new business models, new products, new services, new processes, new roles, new training, and on and on. The whole of business change rests on the ability of an organization to create, and for the organization's members to participate in that creativeness.

Publications and books dealing with creativity range from thought-provoking concepts to scientific-like methods describing the creative process. This section acknowledges the subject of business creativity, individual creativity in business, and the various methods of "being creative" are all worthy subjects to pursue. Rather than broadly cast a net on creativity, this section focuses on the process of engaging others in the creative process. Most organizational change experts would recommend a process that reassembles the ideas presented below—at least in principle.

Roger Von Oech has written several exceptional creativity books. His deck of cards called "Creative Whack Pack" has also proven valuable to me in group situations and for personal brainstorming. Artists will immediately appreciate Mr. Von Oech's books and tools. Once Farmers and Scientists browse the pages of "A Kick in the Seat of the Pants" and "Whack on the Side of the Head", they too will appreciate these creativity stimulators.

This section, along with books and tools similar to those mentioned here, equips the Artist to engage the organization. The guiding principle used for this section is simply to "engage the workforce for their ideas." The Artist is concerned about accessing the organization's collective creativity resulting with executive alignment and organization commitment.

Story: Creativity should not be Limited to the Project Team

An international oil company was putting in field services technology. It was evident there was going to be high resistance from the field operators. There was one individual, however, who was highly respected and had a reputation that went beyond his geographic boundaries in being an excellent operator and an excellent pumper. The challenge was to get him to advocate the technology.

In this instance, I met the gentleman at six o'clock in the morning to go on his route with him, and he looked at me said, "I don't like computers, and I don't like you." He had devised his own processes and his own paperwork and his own methods, and we had essentially finished with his entire route inside of two or three hours. He finished his route in the time it would have taken other people a full day. At the end of his route, I had to honestly tell him that I didn't think that the laptop was going to help him one bit. I had never seen anyone run a route as efficiently as he did.

After my remarks, he asked some very insightful questions and confirmed that a laptop computer would not help him on a daily basis. But by keying in the information every day, he discovered that a laptop would eliminate something he disliked doing on a weekly basis: filing weekly reports that went into the regional office.

By tapping into this man's expertise, a powerful and compelling reason for using the laptop surfaced. Involving him early in the process uncovered a creative way to communicate the laptop's value to others in the field.

Story: Corporate Mavericks as Advocates

For an enterprise-wide application implementation, there were refineries that had been acquired and each of them had built their own processes and used their own computer systems. The corporate organization wanted to have standards for all its refineries. One of the refineries in south Texas always made its numbers and was truly running well, but one of the individuals there had been instrumental in implementing some technology that was outside of the direction that the corporation wanted to go.

It became quite evident that this individual was at risk for throwing up roadblocks and getting in the way of the corporation being able to achieve its goal of having standards across the company. He was a determined maverick. So we simply placed him on the project team to allow him an opportunity to influence the project. By being in the loop, the maverick became one of the corporation's chief advocates for standardization.

Getting people to make commitments to business initiatives is an art. It requires being fair, direct, plain, even blunt, and sometimes even forceful but rarely coercive. Getting people on the team, enlisting people's ideas, coordinating across departments, demonstrating the change—all of this is a way to get people to want to make commitments. They realize that they get to voice their concerns and thus become advocates themselves through their own commitments. The Artist gets stakeholders to participate in a user's wish list or a worker's wish list with the acknowledgment that not all ideas can be used. A good Business Artist also can get people outside of the project to test new processes, new organization designs, and new systems.

Here is an outline the things, which the Artist does to address concerns of commitment and draw out the creativity in others. They are discussed within a framework of overview, considerations, and practices:

- Get More People on the Team
- Coordinate Departments
- Draft User Wish List
- Demonstrate the Change
- Counsel the Stakeholder Groups

Get More People on the Team

Overview: This task gathers multiple disciplines together. Change teams or change groups are formed for specific purposes. Many changes require cooperation between multiple departments and groups. Stakeholder involvement also affects the degree of resistance during change. This task provides an opportunity to address the risks associated with change and creatively derive practical solutions.

Business and technology changes require active participation by multiple disciplines to realize maximum benefit to the organization. This task primarily corresponds to the design and development stages of a business or technology change, but may also apply to the very early stages of conceptual discussion. It provides an opportunity to stimulate cross-functional participation of multiple skills and disciplines.

Considerations: Include multiple support services areas: Facilities, Procurement, IT, HR, Administration, Security, Call Center, and Finance & Accounting. Include multiple line functions as well.

The timing of this task is important. Getting more people involved too early has risks—and certainly, involving people too late has even greater risks. Once the timing of when to bring additional people to the "creative table" is established, it is also important to bring a representative cross-section of talent. Who might have great ideas about the initiative? Who will definitely be able to isolate problem areas that need to be addressed? Who should be part of the selection process to decide upon the additional extended team members? Is there a particular protocol that should be followed?

Practices:

- State to the Farmers and Scientists "This task leverages the talents of support organizations to clarify the degree of commitment and support they can provide, or not provide."
- State to the Farmers and Scientists "This task reduces rework later in the project by getting everyone aligned earlier in the process."
- Make a list of groups, people, areas, and departments affected by the system or business change.
- Make a list showing groups capable of adding a different perspective or area of expertise.
- Contact managers of each group. Convey the nature of the initiative. Identify specific individuals to participate in project.
- Form one or more groups, review teams, advisory committees, or multidiscipline teams.
- Appoint a leader for each team.
- Conduct an overview/introductory meeting with the team members. Provide a synopsis of each person's proposed responsibility.
- Gain estimated level of participation commitment from members.
- Guide each team in the development of a team objective. Objectives should complement the change initiative objectives and blend with project methodologies.
- Schedule specific dates for the groups to meet and work each other. Document findings, results, suggestions, and plans.
- Use teams to plan for actual implementation of the new processes or systems.
- Set up a team-member communication strategy using combinations of voice-mail, internal mail, memorandum, and other methods.

❧

Coordinate Departments

Overview: This task makes sure all departments involved with the change initiative are ready for and aware of the change. Change initiative leader helps the business experts and leaders develop realistic timelines and estimates. All participating departments are integrated. Department coordination and participation are crucial to the success of the project plan.

Considerations: Miscommunication can easily occur between groups. Make sure clear lines of communication are open. Consistently scheduled brief meetings are a good way to be sure information is being communicated on time and to the right people. Groups may want to appoint one person to be their representative for the project. Who is a good communication liaison for the effort? To what degree should managers and supervisors be used to provide this function?

Practices:
- State to the Farmers and Scientists "This task leverages the talent within the organization to accelerate the process."
- Identify all functional areas involved with implementing the change initiative; e.g., Training, Systems, and Human Resources.
- Contact these areas and schedule a meeting to discuss their role(s), availability, schedule, and concerns. Ask participants to identify any conflicts that might arise as a result of the project.
- As a group, agree upon how each group will integrate with all others involved in the change initiative.
- Help each group develop a schedule or timeline that fits into the project as a whole.
- Update the project work plan to include the new timing estimates.

Draft User Wish List

Overview: This task promotes cooperation between systems development personnel and the user community, or between process designers and the business functions being impacted. Blending ideas improves the overall business solution. Systems personnel are more confident in the approach chosen. Process designers become more deeply familiar with the purpose and nature of the work. Impacted personnel and computer users are less resistant upon actual delivery of the system or new process.

Considerations: Systems development efforts especially should include active participation from multiple disciplines. New business process improvements and organizational changes need to also include appropriate business representatives. Management and staff of each stakeholder group should be represented in this task. Who needs to be involved in the design and early discussions? Who would have some creative ideas that are "stretch ideas" to go on a "wish list"?

Practices:

- State to the Farmers and Scientists "This task may find additional good ideas that can be incorporated at low-cost or no-cost."
- Identify individuals from each stakeholder group to participate.
- Construct explanations and diagrams of the proposed technical changes in approachable terms. Avoid technical jargon and diagrams.
- Conduct explanation and idea generation sessions with various groups of the users. Document all suggestions and ideas.
- Evaluate the ideas in terms of the business benefit. Consider the human, organizational, and business process aspects of each idea. Involve appropriate departments.
- Prepare a summary report of all suggestions. Describe and clarify more the ideas to be pursued. Explain why some ideas will not be pursued in this change initiative.

Demonstrate the Change

Overview: Demonstrations can take many forms. Some common forms of demonstrations include a "walk-through", a simulation, watching a prototype in action, a tour of a similar situation, viewing a mock-up or model.

Considerations: When a traditional demonstration is not feasible, the communication events can use stories and hypothetical situations to "demonstrate" the future-state. What are some successful ways demonstrations have been conducted in the past? Who should be involved in giving the demonstration to others? Who is a good sponsor for the demonstrations? Why will some potential participants resist attending a demonstration? What obstacles can be expected and issues related to the demonstration? Who is a skilled facilitator that can help design the demonstration?

Practices:

- State to the Farmers and Scientists "This task provides an overview to key groups, decreasing the risk of finding problems later, and it will also help in the design of future training needs."

- Avoid putting a low-priority on this activity. Many potential future issues can be mitigated through good demonstrations and feedback received.

- Note that this is a "creative" task—this task is not simply to "tell" the participants what is coming, but it also serves to find creative ways that the impacted groups might embrace the changes. This should not be positioned as a training class.

- Decide how the change will be socialized (demonstrations, samples, formal communication vs. informal communication, etc.).

- Preface the demonstration with the limitations of what will be shown and not shown. Providing an overview first will help set the context for the demonstration.

- Decide how success of acceptance will be measured (surveys, informal interviews, focus groups, etc.).

- Monitor acceptance level through feedback.

- If acceptance level is low, try another way to socialize change until acceptance is satisfactory. Follow-up demonstrations may be necessary after adjustments have been made.

Counsel the Stakeholder Groups

Overview: This task deliberately encourages specific dialogue with each group. Ideally, this is a one-on-one sessions and/or small group discussions. Hear stakeholder concerns or points of confusion. Honestly address these points. Regardless of the format, the end-result is to help stakeholders become more open to idea of this specific change. Assume the stakeholder groups and individual will be resilient enough to adapt to the coming changes, and that collectively, they can identify creative ways to make the best of a given situation.

Considerations: For any given "concern" expressed, there are three potential outcomes and remedies: (1) the message was not properly conveyed, or not correctly heard, so the remedy is simply to clarify the message. (2) The message was properly conveyed and received, and the concerns can be directly addressed. The remedy is to change or alter the actions of the project that are causing the concern. (3) The message was properly conveyed and received, but the concerns expressed can not realistically be addressed—and will not be addressed. The remedy is to be truthful. Who is skilled at providing tactful and honest facilitation? What stakeholder groups are most hesitant with the coming change? Why is resistance expected? Why is acceptance expected?

Practices:

- State to the Farmers and Scientists "This task streamlines the largest hurdle in the communication plan—getting key groups on-board."
- Establish the messages and target audiences for this task. Focus on individual impacts. How does change affect the individual?
- Determine the best setting or format for counseling. Some options include: Change Coordinator facilitates a group session. Change Coordinator hosts individual conferences. Supervisors are trained to counsel their staff. Newsletter provides a question/answer column.
- Anticipate and plan for difficult questions.

Creativity Summarized

Creativity is arguably the centerpiece of business change. Business creativity includes the creation of breakthrough business models, new product concepts and almost unimaginable options. This book aims to improve the way business changes are managed, and increase the success rate of PBC initiatives. This book does not intend to explore the many ways human creativity can alter the business landscape. Rather, this section promotes the idea that creativity can, and should, be deliberately "drawn out" of the employees and stakeholder groups facing a PBC. Actively including the various constituents in the process of creating the future changes greatly improves the odds that the groups will eventually embrace and deliver business value in the changes.

The guiding principle used for this section is simply to "engage the workforce for their ideas." Five specific tasks are suggested in this section beginning with the identification and recruitment of adjunct team members to the eventual counseling of all impacted personnel. This way, creative ideas from the rank-and-file work groups and multiple departments contribute to the effort.

The subject of creativity is much broader than the narrow suggestions offered in this book, but these suggestions, when applied, will generally accelerate the success of a PBC. Together with the other four "Cs" of a Business Artist, creativity is an important aspect for the Business Farmer and Business Scientist to encourage.

Capability

A fourth area of interest for Business Artist lies in determining and enhancing organizational capability to achieve an initiative. The variety of alternatives to build capability include traditional classroom instruction, "train-the-trainer" approaches, on-the-job-training, virtual training enabled through technology, self-paced lessons, and many others. A note to the Business Scientists and Business Farmers should be made. Rather than simply default to a particular approach to training and skills capability building, enlisting a professional instructional designer generally pays for itself in several ways—improved quality, efficiency, and total cost. This section includes a checklist appropriate for discovering the high-level training context for a given business change. Even with similar organizations, in similar industries, of similar size, and making similar business changes, the best training approach might vary.

Story: Similar Situations—Different Approaches

This example is about two separate large consumer-goods manufacturers. One firm's headquarters is near Dallas, Texas, and the other in Monterrey, Mexico. Both employed several thousands, and both used route sales people to deliver products to convenience stores, restaurants, grocery stores and other retail establishments.

Both wanted to institute new technology and new processes in their route sales organization, and both were interested in training their newly hired sales employees. In both instances, the approaches adopted worked extremely well and were well received, but they were markedly different.

The Dallas based organization chose to transform what had been a one-week instructor-led program into a three-week structured on-the-job program where new hires were partnered with experienced route salespeople. In the case of the Mexican organization, professional trainers went to the various locations and used a board game that allowed the route salespeople to simulate a route. The game simulated their job, and encouraged competition to see who could sell the most "product" by the end of the game. As part of the game, they used the new technology to experience the business processes in a simulated environment.

In each case, building performance capability was effective. The approach selected was appropriate in both cases, which were nonetheless different from each other.

Clearly, in the example above, differences in the organization's culture, their specific processes, and even the way the companies were organized should have, and did, factor-into the eventual training approach used. The approaches selected were appropriate in both instances. A traditional instructor-led-only approach might have worked, but likely would have been less powerful and more costly in the long-run. This section outlines basics associated with the concept of building employee capability. But, similar to computer systems design, or other engineering disciplines, there are best-practices and techniques associated with the development and delivery of world-class training and employee capability building. Frequently, these skill sets are housed in the Human Resources departments of large companies. In those instances where access to professional instructional designers is difficult, this section provides some basics.

This section would be amiss without mentioning ASTD. The American Society for Training & Development (ASTD) is the world's largest association dedicated to workplace learning and performance professionals. ASTD's 70,000 members and associates come from thousands of organizations. Often, large organizations will have ASTD members among their rank-and-file staff who are not necessarily part of a training department. Drawing out and calling on these individuals out can be beneficial to a PBC.

Great capability building is both a science and an art. The choice to place capability in this section is primarily because the actions are aimed toward the people impacted by the eventual change. Capability is closely associated with the tasks listed in the Creativity and Communication sections above. Below, find tasks outlined to help in the Capability endeavors:

- Define Training Program
- Draft Training Material
- Finalize Training Material
- Make Job Aids
- Deliver Training

Define Training Program

Overview: Training-needs are identified. Current training programs are assessed and missing needs are identified. New skills required to support the change are identified. Course needs are determined and target audiences are examined.

Considerations: Existing training programs should be considered, if applicable. Employees' previous training should provide insight into what type of training is required for each type of change. Enlist the assistance of experienced instructional designers. Who has developed successful training in the past? Why is the training method important? Once the training is delivered, will it ever be used again? What level in the organization does the training target? Are there any language barriers that need to be considered? Will the participants have access to technology, or PCs?

Practices:

- State to the Farmers and Scientists "This task creates a curriculum so the training will be well coordinated, organized, and effective."
- Schedule meeting with training experts or functional experts.
- Prior to the meeting make a rough draft of possible course descriptions and objectives. Define the target audience for proposed training. Define the target audience for proposed training. Write down skills needed by the target audience.
- Consider a variety of training approaches including: (1) Role play, simulation, or in-basket exercise (2) Demonstration presentation (3) Performance tryout (4) Structured discussion/debriefing (5) Case Study (6) Team tasks and group work (7) Brainstorming (8) Panel discussion (9) Structured note taking (10) Field trip and (11) Programmed instructions.
- Gather input regarding the preliminary draft. See if existing materials already exist. Estimate cost of development and delivery.
- Publish a report outlining preliminary findings.
- Gain management approval of the training program prior to actual development of the material/course.

Draft Training Material

Overview: This task sets the standards used for training material. The training technique is finalized (e.g. instructor led, self-paced). The training material packaging options are identified. Use subject matter experts and the training department to assist in determining content and structure. This task includes confirmation of training development cost, training delivery cost, and training support cost. Timelines and schedules should be reviewed and confirmed at this point.

Considerations: Training material standards should be finalized and approved before development begins. Training techniques should be based on audience size and curriculum content. Training content should specifically address the learning and performance objectives. Should corporate communications be involved to review the templates? Are the experts on the team with the development tools that will be used? Can administrative support be enlisted to assist with this effort?

Practices:

- State to the Farmers and Scientists "This task only produces a draft. By making a first draft, we can fine tune the material to meet the specific needs better."
- Schedule meeting with training experts to determine training technique, discuss package options, establish standards for training material, agree on delivery deadlines, make sample document.
- Make sure to comply with any branding requirements, such as use of the company logo.
- Make sure there is adequate access to subject matter experts for defining content.
- Review development status of this task with the training experts and management.
- Provide drafted copies to management for review and approval.

Finalize Training Material

Overview: Final versions of all training materials are produced. Materials are packaged and made ready for delivery.

Considerations: If possible, use the organization's internal print shop organization to lead the final packaging effort. The quantity of training materials needed should be considered. Packaging cost should be approved. Who should be responsible for accomplishing this task, and then delivering the materials to the final destination?

Practices:

- State to the Farmers and Scientists "This task will produce the final training material to be used. Make sure you understand what this is, and how much it will cost so we can move forward."

- Make sure subject matter experts (SME) have reviewed final draft of training materials.
- Obtain management approval of packaging and training technique.
- Reconfirm number of persons to be trained and proposed training calendar.
- Make sure provisions are made for training materials to be duplicated for future needs.
- Distribute materials to appropriate locations. Make special provisions materials that must be delivered to remote locations.

Make Job Aids

Overview: Job-aids are any materials making a job easier. Job-aids are useful to supplement training or to use as a reference while doing work. This task determines if job-aids are needed to make the change initiative successful. Job-aids are developed and distributed.

Considerations: Avoid limiting ideas of job-aids. Job-aids can be anything. Job-aids might include a plastic template, a counting rod, a poster, a recording system. Try not to limit job-aids to paper. Unadvisedly, they can sometimes be expensive and unnecessary. Job-aids are an advantage only if they offer genuine help. Paper-based job-aids may be a good option if the process will be learned and mastered quickly. Creation of job-aids is often a very creative endeavor. Who has experience creating useful job-aids? What areas of the training are the most complex? Why might a job-aid be useful during the training, and after the training?

Practices:
- State to the Farmers and Scientists "This task creates hand-outs that are useful both during the training and after the employees begin the new processes."
- Decide if a job-aid is needed to make the change initiative successful. Ask questions such as: Will a job-aid make an employee more productive? More effective?
- Gather existing documents, notes, or procedures available.
- Brainstorm ideas for potential job-aids. Enlist some creative people, including a graphic artist.
- Make a rough draft of the ideas and ask target audience for feedback.

- Make necessary revisions.
- Arrange appropriate resources and assess how much time is needed to produce job-aids for all employees.
- Gain management approval.
- Coordinate distribution of job-aids with the implementation and training.

Deliver Training

Overview: With the large varieties of training methods available, traditional instructor-led training using in-house trainers or project team members continues to be the most common approach used. Online, web-based training is becoming more prominent. For example, consider including tele-training where a combination of telephone conference-calls are scheduled for remote employees while they review documents or presentations on their PC.

Regardless of the technique selected, schedule participants. Arrange details of training; e.g., resources, and supplies. Deliver training. Collect feedback from participants and prepare to make adjustments to material for future classes.

Considerations: This task is written assuming traditional instructor-led training approaches are used. Other forms of training may be better suited for some change initiatives. Examples of alternatives include tele-training, on-the-job coaching, computer-based training, and simulation environments. When traditional techniques are employed, don't forget breaks and refreshments, if appropriate. Keep focused on objectives and expectations. Identify people who are quick learners who could serve as future mentors on the job. Feedback of participants should be considered for future training. Who are the best people to deliver the training? Are any student/participants candidates to become trainers for future classes?

Practices:

- State to the Farmers and Scientists "Other forms of training could additionally be considered." List other approaches, if appropriate. Continue stating to the Farmers and Scientists "Traditional classroom instruction will be effective, but we need to create a clear schedule, identify trainers, and secure all the resources necessary."
- Compile and finalize list of participants.
- Verify participants have completed prerequisites.
- Reserve space, resources, supplies in advance.

- Consider providing snacks, give-aways, or incentives.
- Communicate intent of training to participants.
- Plan for a brief "get-to-know-each-other" ice-breaker session.
- Review course objectives, expectations, and time frame with participants.
- Plan for breaks every 45 to 90 minutes.
- Have a recap session.
- Get feedback.
- Make improvements to future classes based on the feedback.
- Send a thank you note for coming.

Capability Summarized

Exceptional training development is both a science and an art. Enlisting the skills of a professional instructional designer is advised. Beyond that recommendation, the creative development process and delivery of training to build employee capability is closely associated with communication, culture, and core HR. Hence, capability is included in this section for the Business Artist.

Many varieties exist to build employee capability during a business change. These include traditional classroom instruction, train-the-trainer approaches, on-the-job-training, virtual training enabled through technology, self-paced lessons, and many others. This section provides a starting-point for identification of possible options, along with the tasks typically involved in designing and delivering capability training.

A specific suggestion to consider the development of job-aids, and enlisting the creative talents of the organization—especially those of a graphic artist—is recommended for larger changes. For the case study presented which included two large consumer goods organizations, graphic artists were used to produce the final job-aids to support the training. In both instances, this decision proved wise. Business Farmers and Business Scientists understandably might resist the additional investment in time and/or money to use a professional graphic artist. For large initiatives, it frequently will make sense both to improve quality, and in the long-run for total time spent (cost) to produce the end-product. Small, less complex initiatives can be managed without this luxury.

Training (capability building) is frequently housed in the Human Resources department of larger organizations. Appropriately, the next and final section reviews the Business Artist's perspective on Core HR.

Core HR

The fifth and final area of interest for Business Artist is in Core Human Resources. Human Resources can be both a "farming" and "scientific" endeavor. Certainly, many laws apply to the Human Resources function, and policies related to employment are issued from the HR department. The placement of Core HR in the Artist section centers on the attention and effect that Core HR has on the employee population. In particular, the manner in which jobs are defined, job relationships are arranged, and the way an organization is designed all influence the behaviors of individuals with other parts of their organization.

This section is written from an Artists viewpoint, whereas Core HR has the ability to influence the behaviors and acceptance of impacted stakeholder groups and individual employees during a PBC.

The US Department of Labor Bureau of Labor Statistics provides current, public-domain information about the job market, along with excellent detailed descriptions of hundreds of job types.

For those interested in more deeply exploring the way the Human Resource function can influence the success of a PBC, consider looking into the Society for Human Resource Management (SHRM). SHRM is the world's largest association devoted to human resource management, representing more than 200,000 individual members. The Society's mission is to advance the human resource profession to ensure that HR is recognized as an essential partner in developing and executing organizational strategy.

Also, the Human Resource Certification Institute (HRCI) provides professional certification to HR professionals. Since 1976, more than 53,000 HR professionals have been certified through this organization.

Here is an outline of five things the Artist considers with regard to Core-HR. As with discussions in the metaphorical role of the Farmer and Scientist, each is discussed within a framework of overview, considerations, and practices:
- List Basic Job Functions

- Identify Job Relationships
- Draft Job Descriptions
- Find Organization Design Opportunity
- Identify Human Resource Programs

List Basic Job Functions

Overview: This task summarizes functions and responsibilities of a new job or an altered role. It is also used to update or modify the responsibilities of an existing job. Subject Matter Experts are required to participate in this task. This task involves identification of job (or role) objectives, functions, responsibilities, and authority.

Considerations: Enlist HR professionals for this task. Factor-in organization goals when determining basic job functions. Job attributes need to be considered. Examples include degree of autonomy, meaningfulness of work, employee empowerment, vertical and horizontal responsibilities. Example job design strategies include job simplification, job growth, job enrichment, and autonomous work groups. Who is an expert in this area?

Practices:

- State to the Farmers and Scientists "This task lists the jobs impacted by the changes, and identifies differences between jobs that sound the same but may not actually be the same."
- Enlist Human Resources, or a job design expert to lead this process.
- Determine what the job is to accomplish, the job objectives.
- Draft an overview of the basic job functions.
- Obtain management approval.

Identify Job Relationships

Overview: Job relationships for business units are described and analyzed. Suggestions are made for realignment of organizational structure. This task can be complex. Involvement of Human Resources and job design experts may be required.

Considerations: An inappropriate organization structure creates conflict and confusion among units and members, poor resource utilization, and ineffective work environments. Appropriate structure provides role clarity, efficient resource utilization, appropriate flexibility, and effective communication. Who would be resistant to altering the structure?

Practices:

- State to the Farmers and Scientists "This task makes sure the appropriate amount of supervision is in place within the organization for all the key processes."
- Consider requirements in place related to a unionized workforce and comply with those requirements, if applicable.
- Assess job relationships for business units. Consider these factors: role clarity, resource utilization, and inefficiencies.
- Identify existing methods of communication between job types. Ensure effective communication principals are identified for all jobs.
- Identify horizontal organization of the business unit. Horizontal components usually equate to business processes. Consider autonomy, coordination between jobs, and culture.
- Identify vertical organization of the business unit. Vertical design focuses on aligning people to perform management processes such as planning, communication, and allocation.
- Use job design experts to approve work done in this task.

Draft Job Descriptions

Overview: This task identifies crucial skills, abilities, and behaviors needed to perform a job. Key Performance Indicators are identified for each job or role. Final drafts are consistent with organization job description standards.

Considerations: Job descriptions are specific. Care must be taken to consider all important activities and skills. New job descriptions may require new workspace, new performance appraisal system, or new work force structure. All of these areas must be aligned with the vision, the organizational structure, and the target culture. Job design experts and Human Resource experts should help in this task. Who can be enlisted to lead this task?

Practices:

- State to the Farmers and Scientists "This task writes out the job description for key roles."
- Identify job to be described. Review results from previous analysis.
- Confirm activities performed and skills required.
- For new jobs, list activities, competencies and skills required.
- Get feedback from a job design expert.
- Make necessary revisions.

- Design/develop key performance indicators (KPIs).
- Get approval of key performance from management.
- Publish description in a format consistent with organization standards.

Find Organization Design Opportunity

Overview: This task encourages analysis of the current state roles, responsibility, and reporting structure within a business unit. This task is not meant to be a large-scale reorganization event. Rather, improved collaborative processes deserve acknowledgment that a few new "roles" will likely emerge and a few traditional roles might change in their charter.

Considerations: Enlist Human Resource professionals during this task, which includes organization structure and incentives. There are several techniques that establish organization structure or organization design. An excellent model shows five different ways by which to organize: geography, process, function, market, and product. "Designing Organizations: An Executive Briefing on Strategy, Structure, and Process" by James R. Galbraith is my favorite text on this subject.

Organization design includes roles, responsibilities, and reporting relationships. Here, see an illustration of the relationship of job role and job responsibility area.

Same role, different responsibility
- Sales job "A" is responsible for selling to clients in Texas.
- Sales job "B" is responsible for selling to clients in California.

These two jobs are identical, except they are responsible for clients in different geographies.

Same responsibility area, different role
- Sales job "A" is responsible for selling to clients in Texas.
- Finance job "C" is responsible for maintaining financial transactions related to Texas clients.

These two jobs are different, but they share responsibility for the same part of the business.

Both situations happen frequently in organizations of all types. For these illustrations, job "A" and "B" could both report to a Sales Manager. In contrast, job "A" and "C" could report to a Regional Manager for Texas. Both organization designs are valid and can work. Both designs have strengths and weaknesses. HR can assist in developing the positives and negatives of various organizational designs.

Who needs to be included in the definition of roles, responsibilities, and reporting relationships? Is there a need to increase or decrease the number of individuals performing a particular role?

Practices:

- State to the Farmers and Scientists "This task uses the high-level estimates of workload to balance with the number of people and roles within the impacted organization."
- Gather the current roles, reporting relationships, responsibilities.
- Identify goals and intentions of the business unit, or group.
- Compare how the current-state organization enables the goals.
- Identify potential, alternative organizing constructs; e.g., by market segment, major process, geography, function, product/service.
- Use newly drafted role descriptions and reporting structures to estimate number of staff required to fill each role.
- Draft a synopsis of the results along with recommendations.
- Select a path-forward and plan for implementation.

Identify Human Resource Programs

Overview: This task identifies HR programs supporting the change initiative. HR experts are informed of changes taking place. HR is consulted and included in the development of new programs to accommodate change initiatives. Changes in HR processes can be complex; e.g., forecast, recruit, develop, evaluate, reward, progress, retain, and retire.

Considerations: Accommodation of human resource issues is crucial to the change process. By answering questions such as, "Will the system meet both organizational and employee needs?" this task can link the culture of organization with change. Job design experts and Human Resource experts are recommended to perform this task. How can HR programs support new employee behaviors?

Practices:

- State to the Farmers and Scientists "This task makes sure the project complies with any applicable Human Resources requirements we might not otherwise know about."
- Reach agreement regarding the need to address HR issues.
- Recruiting
- New hire training
- Compensation

- Bonus and other awards programs
- Career paths
- Performance reviews
- Promotions
- Job sharing, job enrichment
- Separation and severance
- Use the organization's HR tools as they are available.
- Work with the experts to design appropriate programs. For example, consider areas such as performance appraisal, compensation, and recruiting.

Core HR Summarized

This section focuses on the manner in which HR can influence the behaviors and acceptance by the impacted employees during a PBC. For this reason Core HR is included in the Business Artist section, along with the related Business Artist perspectives of Culture, Communication, Creativity and Capability.

The entire life cycle of employee relations may influence the success of a PBC:

- Forecasting needs
- Recruiting talent
- Developing capability
- Evaluating performance
- Rewarding results
- Progressing, retaining, and separating from employees

In particular, the tasks associated with organizational design are applicable in many PBCs. Enlisting the HR function, or other job-design experts to assist in these tasks can be very helpful. Outlined in this section were generalized guidelines to identify and define jobs, define job relationships and estimate staffing needs and requirements. Alterations in the design of jobs, roles, reporting relationships and staffing levels can result in confusion, resistance, and other emotions. Because of this, it is appropriate to perform many Core HR activities concurrently with the Business Artist's activities.

Artist Summarized

Several job titles tend to perform Business Artist activities even though any given individual working on a business change may have an affinity toward the role of Artist. Business strategists, communication specialists, graphic artists, several human resources roles, and some marketing disciplines tend to perform as Business Artists during PBC.

Business Artists as described in this book draw from their ability to work with people, influence employee behavior, and contribute business results from these activities. Their areas of interest include corporate culture, change enabling communication, creative processes, building staff capability through training, and many core human resources activities.

Business Artists are visionary and creative. They seek imaginative ways to increase profit. They gravitate toward abstractions, concepts, models, and taxonomies. Business Artists find ways to apply concepts from otherwise seemingly unrelated industries to their own organization.

The importance of the "people factor" in successful business change is underscored by the recent development of the People Capability Maturity Model® referenced earlier.

The primary recommendation to Business Artists in this book is for the Artist to speak about concrete actions and concrete business results when interacting with Scientists and Farmers. Each task listed under Business Artist suggested a way to express the task to Farmers and Scientists. Using the suggested language will reduce the possibility of having the "Art" eliminated from a project plan. Using the concrete language will resonate with the Scientist project managers and be appreciated by the practical Farmers, and less likely to be viewed as "extra" or a luxury.

An illustration toward the front of the book described that an artist would consider the alternate possibilities of a broken fence, whereas the Scientist would think in terms of "how" to properly fix the fence. In particular, the artist might wonder "who" needs the fence and "why" is the fence needed? The idea that Artists are interested in "the-who" and "the-why" during PBC is described further in each of the Five-Cs:

- Culture
- Communication
- Creativity
- Capability
- Core HR

Each of these areas were described by using the framework of overview, considerations, and practices (what, who/why, and how/when) in the language of Farmer, Artist, and Scientist, respectively.

By reviewing the Five-Cs, business change participants are better equipped to discuss an initiative with an Artist, and Artists are better able to translate their needs to Scientists and Farmers.

With this, the three major roles of Farmer, Scientist and Artist have been described.

❧

Part 7

Hybrid Perspectives

The three basic roles have been reviewed and provide the basis for better understanding the perspectives of various team members and constituent stakeholder groups impacted by the PBC. Figures 3 through 5 illustrate how the three roles also intersect with each other.

The three intersection areas include Farmer-Scientist, Artist-Farmer, and Scientist-Artist. These three hybrid perspectives can be described as: Program Manager, Sales Entrepreneur, and Business Inventor, respectively. PBC frequently emphasizes two of the three basic roles, in these hybrid forms, while failing to attend to the third role. Some PBC will succeed with attention to two roles, producing business benefit. However, the maximum business benefit will rarely be achieved without all three primary perspectives. This section discusses the characteristics and risks of PBC attending to only two of the three primary roles.

Program Manager

This hybrid perspective blends the viewpoint of Farmer and Scientist. Largely excluded from this perspective is the Artist role. For organizations whose value discipline is operational excellence, the perspective of Farmer-Scientist is highly valued. Here, the Farmer's emphasis on business objectives and the Scientist's attention toward planning merge.

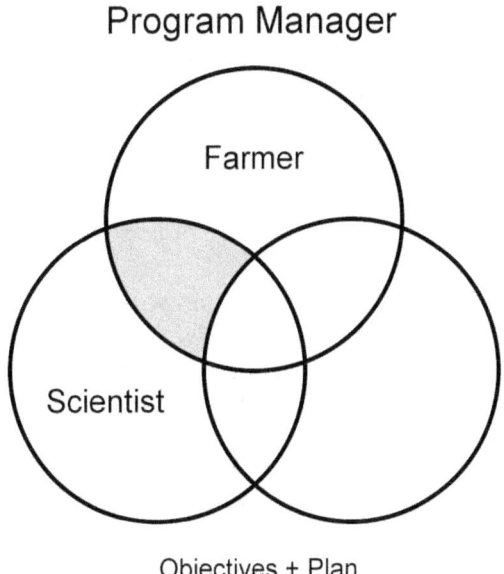

Figure 3: Program Manager Hybrid.

Engineering and manufacturing organizations frequently celebrate this perspective, and for good reason. Organizations operating on thin margins, strict deadlines, or with complex initiatives absolutely need to emphasize the Farmer and the Scientist roles. This is a powerful combination for large-scale change. Most large management consulting organizations have recognized this perspective as extremely important when delivering work to their clients.

Command-and-control, meticulous time-tracking, authority of discretionary budget, and best-practices associated with project management (such as Earned Value concepts) are very important to teams made up exclusively of Farmers and Scientists. Still, the best Program Management perspective includes room for Artist contributions. The Program Management perspective that entirely ignores the Artist may deliver the initiative on time and on budget, but the ignored people-issues may be a cost burden after-the-fact.

For example, an initiative may be fully delivered on paper, but the users of the new computer application may not be using advanced features that are built-in to the application. In this example, the users may eventually be trained in the advanced features. During the interim though, there is an untracked opportunity cost from inefficient usage, and the follow-up training is accounted for as part of the on-going support cost at a later time. Worse yet, end-users of the application may become frustrated and abandon the new system, or begin creating spreadsheets or other rouge tracking systems and processes.

The lists below summarize characteristics and business risks of a Program Manager emphasis without the Artist role included in the effort.

Characteristics
- **Structured.** Bureaucratic, command and control orientation.
- **Methodical.** Disciplined teamwork with a process focus, typically following a prescriptive methodology.
- **Standardized.** Conformance throughout the initiative, where policies and procedures are enforced and adhered to from all team members.
- **Scheduled.** Centralized Project Management Office with scheduled weekly meetings of key team leaders.
- **Expertise.** Team leaders are viewed as having high skills within their area of expertise (Scientists).
- **Efficiency.** Notably, this hybrid orientation works best with business transformations seeking to lower cost and increase organizational efficiency.

Business Risks
- **Over optimism.** False assumptions that independent operating units are complying with, or will comply with the initiative's intention and outcome

- **Missed opportunities.** Overlook easier quick-hit opportunities that can yield high return with little-to-no cost and effort
- **Talent loss.** High turn-over of experienced employees in the impacted areas, especially during an up-market where key skills are sought and heavily recruited
- **Deferred cost.** Hidden down-stream cost associated with re-training staff or ineffective use of new processes and technology
- **Rouge organizations.** Resistant groups create duplicate processes to fit their specific needs.

Sales Entrepreneur

This hybrid perspective blends the viewpoint of Artist and Farmer. Largely excluded from this perspective is the Scientist role. For organizations whose value discipline is customer intimacy, this perspective is highly valued. Intersecting here are the Artist's ability to communicate and the Farmer's vision for business opportunity.

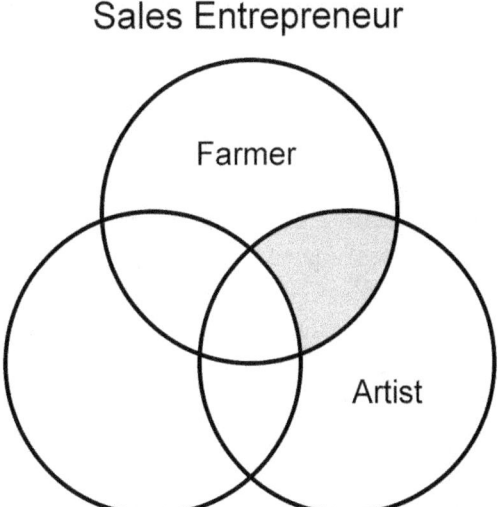

Figure 4: Sales Entrepreneur Hybrid.

Many professional service organizations celebrate this perspective because of the relationship of external sales and marketing functions with internal operations. Organizations dependent on deep customer knowledge to create breakthrough insights ahead of competition need this hybrid perspective. Similar to the Program Manager perspective, the Sales Entrepreneur perspective is a powerful advantage for organizations valuing their alignment with customer needs.

With the Sales Entrepreneur perspective, phrases like "business solution" and "stakeholder group" are commonly used to describe ideas and concepts. Standardization opportunities typically take a back to the possibilities of creating specific results and solutions for important market segments or particular internal organizational units.

A team made up of Farmer's and Artists, without their Scientist colleagues will gravitate toward the Sales Entrepreneur perspective. Together, they may design, develop and deliver exceptional value to the various stakeholder groups. But, without including an appropriate level of Scientist-thinking, the effort to reach the end-result may be inefficient with continual iterations of re-do, re-packaging, and re-design. Also common to this scenario is inadequate attention to how to sustain and manage the change once it is in place.

The lists below summarize the characteristics and business risks of a Sales Entrepreneur emphasis without the Scientist role included in the effort.

Characteristics

- **Customer focused.** Substantial emphasis on user requirements, customer requirements, and segmentation of those various needs.
- **Solution oriented.** A focus toward solutions tailored for particular important stakeholder groups (either internal or external).
- **Results driven.** Attention on the business results, with much less attention toward how those results are achieved.
- **Energized.** Excitement and anticipation of something "new" is generated and communicated frequently, with active gathering and analysis of feedback.
- **Empowering.** A general belief that decision making can be delegated without bureaucratic-like processes.

Business Risks

- **Missed deadlines.** Inadequate planning on the front-end results in missed target dates and disappointed customers (both internal and external).
- **Confusion.** Some key decisions get delayed because of "too many cooks in the kitchen."
- **Complexity.** Too many solutions are unmanageable and impractical to put into action.

- **Endless re-work.** Seemingly endless iterations of design cause fatigue and frustration to team members.
- **Unsustainable design.** Overlooking details related to day-to-day transactions and how to sustain the new solution after it is implemented.

Business Inventor

This final hybrid perspective blends the viewpoint of Scientist and Artist, the Business Inventor. Largely excluded from this perspective is the Farmer role. For organizations whose value discipline is innovation of new products or services, this perspective is highly valued. Here, Scientist's ability to experiment through prototyping and the Artist's creativity merge together.

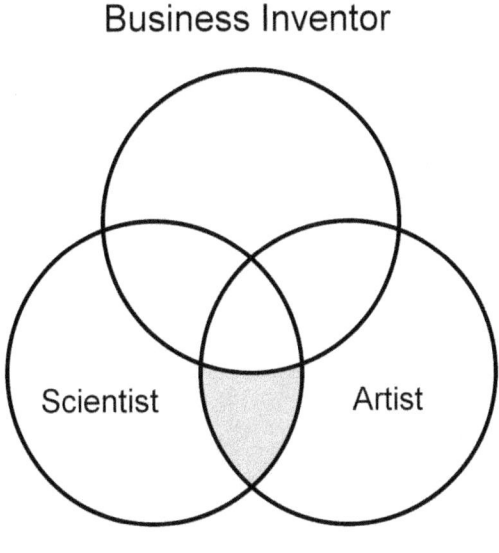

Prototype + Creativity

Figure 5: Business Inventor Hybrid.

For example, some consumer product organizations may celebrate this perspective. Any organization with a culture of business innovation and creativity may tend to over-emphasize this perspective during a PBC.

The Business Inventor perspective is a powerful advantage for organizations dependent on quickly commercializing new ideas, or discovery of new products that can leapfrog their competition. Phrases like "time-to-market" are common in teams with the Business Inventor perspective. These teams are comfortable with experimentation, out-of-the-box thinking, and imagination of what might be possible.

Project teams staffed with Artists and Scientists will quickly embrace the Business Inventor perspective. Together, they may deliver awesome new products with incredible speed. Without the big-picture view of a Farmer, the result may have no commercial application though it is interesting or even technically fascinating.

Notably, in organizations where innovation is not a core competency, project teams comprised only of Scientists and Artists run the highest risk of launching a suspect business change as described earlier in this book. Suspect change has little-to-no probability of yielding business benefit.

The lists below summarize the characteristics and business risks of a Business Inventor emphasis without the Farmer role included in the effort.

Characteristics
- **Conceptual.** Ability to conceptualize and test several creative alternatives or break-through ideas.
- **Imaginative.** Imagination of what the market or internal organizations might appreciate if these groups only knew what was possible.
- **Fast.** Saleable concepts ahead of the market.
- **Flexible.** Flexible team members willing to switch hats and play multiple roles.
- **Undeterred.** Celebration of failures and success. Failure is simply viewed as one step closer to success.

Business Risks
- **Wheel-Spinning.** Ever-changing business requirements not tied to a particular set of objectives.
- **Poor corporate fit.** Spending time, effort, and resources on ideas that don't fit the corporate purpose, function, or vision.
- **No cost control.** Cavalier or naive disregard for cost or obligations, building up overruns.
- **Pollyanna attitude.** An unrealistic assumption that everything will eventually come out all right, and not thinking through contingencies for failure.

Part 8

Change Agent

"We must learn to live together as brothers or perish together as fools." Martin Luther King Jr.

"Success doesn't come to you...you go to it." Marva N. Collins.

Throughout history, there have been extraordinary individuals who have dramatically influenced entire societies, and influenced our culture for decades and even centuries later. This book has humbler aspirations than this. Still, these powerful examples provide the basis for an aspiring business Change Agent to set sail. Of the thousands of business changes launched each day, many do not have their Change Agent. Many initiatives will either fail or miss their full potential. Other initiatives will thrive—their business Change Agent recognizes the importance of "living together as brothers" and that we must "go to" the success rather than wait for it to arrive.

The Change Agent understands and communicates well with the Business Farmer, Business Scientist, and Business Artist. The Change Agent may have a personal affinity toward one of the three primary roles described in this book, but is able to adjust his or her perspective to fit the situation and discussion at hand. The Change Agent is a central figure in the business improvement process. Any participant in a business change can practice *being* a Change Agent, and work toward *leading* as a Change Agent.

Because this book aims to improve the way business changes are managed, an objective of this book is to encourage some business change participants to consider the value of being a Change Agent rather than a change participant only.

This achievement will be evident when the change participant:

Summarizes the "five-Os" during a PBC to the Business Farmers through an overview.

Identifies and advocates the use of best practices and the "five-Ps" with the Business Scientists.

Engages with the Business Artists through consideration of the "five-Cs".

We have reviewed that PBC serves to provoke, excite, or stimulate discussion, resistance and controversy. Further, an estimated 75% of business projects, programs, and major initiatives each year in major organizations fit this category. A PBC tends to result in a fundamental change in the effectiveness or approach of the organization. These initiatives include process improvement, reengineering, supply chain initiatives, enterprise resource planning (ERP), customer relationship management (CRM), enterprise technology, Six-Sigma or quality projects, and many operations improvements. Participation in these initiatives with an understanding of the perspective of the Business Farmer, Scientist and Artist will improve the chance of a successful business change.

This book focuses on business changes that have likely business benefit, but are only one of perhaps several dozen alternatives that could-be initiated for the intended benefit. These business changes are not required but are still often extremely important for the long-term viability of the organization. But, it is rare that all impacted groups and participants would immediately agree with a particular initiative's intentions and approach. So while PBC provokes excitement, it is also reasonable to expect resistance, and even controversy. Ideas expressed in this book might apply to business imperatives, change required from regulation, or even the unprofitable suspect change. But, the focus of this book and its lessons are toward PBC. If this book serves to influence a change participant toward practicing seeing through the eyes of the Farmer, Scientist, and Artist, it will have served its purpose.

Change Agent

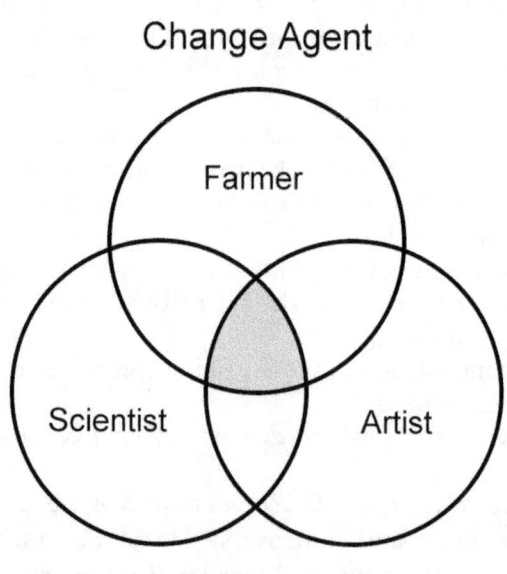

Overview + Considerations + Practices

Figure 6: Change Agent.

A single text can not reasonably review all the possibilities, nuances, and perspectives of individuals, corporate cultures, and business approaches. Still, the idea that there are three general perspectives as outlined herein has proven valuable to me during my participation with dozens of organization's change efforts over the past twenty years. These insights and considerations represent a composite of practices from leading business change consulting organizations, and hundreds of client executives, managers, and staff.

Regardless of whether one feels inclined to become a Change Agent as described in this book, the suggestions to each of the three primary roles remain valid.

To the Farmer: Get in the wheelbarrow.

To the Scientist: Use less technical jargon.

To the Artist: Speak about actions and concrete results.

And last...

To the Change Agent: Happy Business-Turfing™!

Part 9

Glossary and Lists

Visit www.businessturfing.com for additional supplementary information, beyond the glossary and lists provided here.

This glossary serves as a reference to readers of this book, and as a quick tool to interpret commonly used acronyms during Provocative Business Change™. Web links related to topics and organizations referenced in this book are also listed in alphabetical order.

Glossary

ABC—a technique. Activity Based Costing. This accounting technique calculates and assigns cost to activities or business processes. For example, in the banking industry, this technique could identify the cost of processing a customer's check. For an electric utility, this technique could calculate the total cost involved in printing and sending a hard-copy bill. ABC finds the actual total cost associated with a product, service, or process performed by an organization without regard to the organizational structure. ABC is applicable to any industry, any business process, and any product or service. While ABC can be a powerful management tool, the technique remains somewhat difficult to perform in many organizations and is not yet widely practiced.

AICPA—an organization. The American Institute of Certified Public Accountants (AICPA) communicates accounting standards to its members, and provides a self-governing oversight-like function for the accounting professional code of conduct.

AIPMM—an organization. The Association of International Product Marketing Managers provides certification for marketing product managers. The Certified Product Manager™ (CPM) and Certified Product Marketing Manager™ (CPMM) credentials cross industry barriers, focusing on marketing best practices and strategic skills.

APICS—an organization. The Association for Operations Management was originally founded in 1958 and originally known as American Production and Inventory Control Society. The acronym, APICS, was a widely recognized brand when the mission and name change were later put into effect. The organization chose to retain the recognizable acronym while changing the official name to better reflect attention toward service organizations in addition to manufacturing organizations.

APQC — an organization. The American Productivity & Quality Center began in 1977 with the backing of leaders from several Fortune 1000 companies, union heads, and former senior government officials. Today, APQC is an internationally recognized resource for process and performance improvement assisting organizations to adapt to changing environments with new and better ways to work. Among the notable achievements, APQC spearheaded the creation and design of the Malcolm Baldrige National Quality Award™ in 1987.

ASTD — an organization. American Society for Training & Development is the world's largest association dedicated to workplace learning and performance professionals. ASTD's members have access to several substantial databases, discussion boards, and best practice repositories online, as well as access to local and regional expert groups interested in the subjects of training and professional development.

BPI — a technique. Business Process Improvement refers to an intentional effort to evolve the way work is performed to reduce cost or increase profit. BPI is a broad topic that is at various times relates to each of the following phrases prefaced with business process (BP): BP analysis, BP architectural modeling, BP assessment, BP design, BP development, BP engineering, BP flow management, BP reengineering, BP indicator, BP integration, BP management, BP management systems, BP manual, BP maturity model, BP modeling, BP object, BP optimization, BP outsourcing, and BP procedure.

CEO — a job title. The Chief Executive Officer is the corporate executive ultimately responsible for all financial, legal, and operational aspects of an organization, reporting to a board of directors. The CEO frequently appoints other managers.

CFO — a job title. The Chief Financial Officer is the corporate executive having financial authority to make appropriations and authorize expenditures for a firm. The CFO leads the organization's finance and accounting functions, and sometimes leads other related functions or departments.

CMMI — a technique. Capability Maturity Model® Integration (CMMI) is a process improvement approach identifying the essential elements of an effective process. The practices guide project teams, departments, or an entire organization to set process improvement goals and priorities. CMMI is an outcome of efforts by the Software Engineering Institute, which is a federally funded research and development center operated by Carnegie Mellon University and sponsored by the U.S. Department of Defense.

COO — a job title. The Chief Operating Officer is the corporate executive responsible for the operations of the firm; reporting to the CEO. The COO may at times appoint other managers.

CRM — a technology. In this book, CRM always refers to Customer Relationship Management. CRM is used to abbreviate over fifty business concepts that are not related to customer relationship management at all. Some examples of these include computer resource management, compliance research and measurement, and cause related marketing. Customer relationship management refers to a large number of application software solutions providing data entry, and other sophisticated functions pertaining to customers, marketing efforts, and sales promotions. This acronym can be confusing without establishing which meaning of CRM is intended. Business Scientists should take care to clearly establish context and explanation of which meaning of "CRM" is being discussed.

CRP — a technology. Capacity Requirements Planning in the book refers to application software associated with a manufacturing facility intended to estimate the capacity, or absence of capacity to fulfill production demands. This acronym is often confusing because CRM abbreviates over seventy common three-word-expressions in business. Some examples of these alternative phrases include: Certified Recovery Planner, Child-Resistant Packaging, and Common Resource Pool. Business Scientists should take care to clearly establish context and explanation of which meaning of "CRP" is being discussed.

DMAIC — a technique. DMAIC (pronounced "Duh-MAY-ick") is a problem-solving method. The letters are an acronym for the five phases of a Six-Sigma improvement effort: Define-Measure-Analyze-Improve-Control. Organizations which have adopted Six-Sigma frequently have employees certified with the designations of Black Belt and Green Belt.

ERP — a technology. ERP in this book always refers to application software known generically as Enterprise Resource Planning. Sixty other variations and uses of the acronym ERP are used in various business disciplines, which have nothing to do with Enterprise Resource Planning. Some examples include: Exchange Rate Policies, Estimated Retail Price, and Error Recovery Procedure. In practice, ERP software may include the majority of an organization's departments, functions, and major business processes. ERP may include manufacturing software, financial software, human resources software, and other functions. Many organizations have an ERP system installed for their finance and accounting department only (for example), whereas other organizations may use the same vendor's ERP modules for their supply chain and manufacturing operations. Business Scientists should take care to clearly establish context and explanation of which meaning of "ERP" is being discussed, as well as the business functions being managed with the ERP system.

FTE—a unit of measure. Full Time Equivalent refers to an amount of time. If one person works full time for one year, then that equals one FTE for that year. If two people work half-time for a full year, that too equals one FTE for that year. A third example would be if one person works full time for the first half of the year, and a second person works full time the second half of the year, that also equals one FTE for that year. Project managers commonly use this term to refer to the number of *hours* their team members will be dedicating to an effort during a fixed length of time. More than twenty alternate meanings of FTE are used in business, including: Facilities, Terminals, and Equipment, Factory Test Equipment, and Fully Taxable Equivalent. Business Scientists should take care to clearly establish context and explanation of which meaning of "FTE" is being discussed.

HR—a department. Human Resource departments within an organization are responsible for the people processes and obligations of the firm. Beyond compliance with legal requirements related to employers and employees, these processes include forecasting needs of staff, recruiting staff, developing and evaluating employees, compensating and rewarding employees, retention efforts as well as employee separation and severance processes.

HRCI—an organization. Human Resource Certification Institute (HRCI) provides professional certification to HR professionals. Since 1976, more than 53,000 HR professionals have been certified through this organization.

ISO—an organization. The International Organization for Standardization is the world's largest developer of standards. Several other business phrases are abbreviated with ISO, including: Inspection of Services, Information Security Officer, and Internet Sales Outlet. Business Scientists should take care to clearly establish context and explanation of which meaning of "ISO" is being discussed.

IT—a department. Information Technology is a function within an organization providing the installation and subsequent support of communications equipment, computer hardware, applications software and related items. While the acronym IT is widely understood to mean information technology, there are over fifty alternate business and professional phrases that also use the acronym. For example:

In Transition, Income Tax, Individual Training, Inflation Target, Informational Theory, Investment Trust, and Interstitial Transfer. Business Scientists should take care to clearly establish which meaning of "IT" is being discussed.

KPI — a unit of measure. Key Performance Indicators are a set of quantifiable measures that an organization uses to gauge or compare performance in terms of meeting their strategic and operational goals. KPIs vary between organizations and industries, depending on their priorities or performance criteria. Sometimes these are also referred to as "key success indicators (KSI)".

MRP — a technology. Materials Resource Planning refers to application software primarily used with manufacturing organizations. In this book MRP is used only to refer to Materials Resource Planning. In business and professional venues, MRP may alternatively be used to abbreviate over thirty common expressions including: Mid-Range Plan, Maintenance Recovery Period, Manufacturer's Recommended Price, and Most Reliable Path. Business Scientists should take care to clearly establish which meaning of "MRP" is being discussed.

PBC — a category. Provocative Business Change™ serves to provoke, excite, or stimulate discussion, resistance and controversy. An estimated 75% of business projects, programs, and major initiatives each year in major organizations fit this category. If adopted within an organization as an abbreviation, it should be noted that PBC is also used for over twenty other business expressions including: Pay by Computer, Postal Business Center, and Prepared by Client. Business Scientists should take care to clearly establish which meaning of "PBC" is being discussed.

PMI — an organization. The Project Management Institute provides authoritative and widely recognized certification for project managers. Over thirty other business and professional expressions are abbreviated with the acronym PMI including: Pre-Market Indicator, Private Mortgage Insurance, and Pensions Management Institute. Business Scientists should take care to clearly establish which meaning of "PMI" is being discussed.

PMO — a team. Program Management Office, or Project Management Office, is a group of professionals who have oversight of one or more significant projects or business change efforts. PMO also serves as an abbreviation for phrases such as Present Method of Operation, Preventive Medicine Officer, and Plant Maintenance Order. Business Scientists should take care to clearly establish which meaning of "PMO" is being discussed.

ROI—a unit of measure. Return on investment is typically expressed as a percentage. ROI is used as a financial unit of measure for the purpose of making business decisions. ROI calculations require knowledge of cost and benefit of an action. While ROI almost always means Return on Investment during a business change conversation, there are a few alternate meanings of ROI including: Record of Invention, Radius of Influence, and RAM Optical Instrumentation. Business Scientists should establish which meaning of "ROI" is being discussed

SDLC—a technique. Systems Development Life Cycle is the process of developing information systems through investigation, analysis, design, implementation, and maintenance. Using SDLC should result in a high quality system that meets or exceeds customer expectations, within time and cost estimates, works effectively and efficiently in the current and planned information technology environment. Sometimes SDLC is used to mean *Software* Development Life Cycle, which is essentially the same thing.

SEI—an organization. Software Engineering Institute is a federally funded research and development center sponsored by the U.S. Department of Defense and operated by Carnegie Mellon University.

SHRM—an organization. Society for Human Resource Management is the world's largest association devoted to human resource management. SHRM aims to advance the human resource profession. Except for the single occurrence within the construction industry of "Saw Horse Roof Mount" I am not aware of another usage for this acronym.

SME—an individual. The expression Subject Matter Expert very nearly approximates this book's description of a Business Scientist. The acronym is also used to abbreviate Sales Management Engineer, Security Message Exchange, Spatial Modeling Environment, and Systems Maintenance Engineer, as well as other phrases.

SMEI—an organization. Sales & Marketing Executives International is a worldwide knowledge-growth and relationship-building forum created primarily for sales and marketing executives. It has over fifty affiliate chapters around the world. Care with this acronym is appropriate because at times it is used to refer to a Small/Medium Enterprise Initiative.

ॐ

Web Links
Several information sources and references to important organizations were made in this book. Below, find the web address

of these sources and organizations. Many of these are referenced or further described from www.businessturfing.com.

www.accenture.com
www.aicpa.org
www.aipmm.com
www.ansi.org
www.apics.org
www.apqc.org
www.astd.org
www.balancedscorecard.org
www.bls.gov
www.businessturfing.com
www.brint.com
www.capgemini.com
www.copyright.gov
www.csc.com
www.georgegroup.com
www.gsb.stanford.edu
www.hrci.org
www.iso.org
www.marketingpower.com
www.mit.edu
www.nssn.org
www.pmi.org
www.sei.cmu.edu
www.shrm.org
www.smei.org
www.sogeti-transiciel.com
www.uspto.gov

Stories and Illustrations

This list summarizes the stories and illustrations used throughout the book. Most of these stories are from first-hand experience and observation. For the remaining stories, care was taken to not specifically reveal an individual or organization name except where information is publicly available. For the nineteenth century stories of George Blondin and E.I. Du Pont, care was taken to accurately depict these powerful stories as much as possible through research. In particular, the Brandywine River Museum was helpful in validating the story of Mr. Du Pont.

Types of Business Change
Defending Against Hostile Take-Over
Unsolicited Acquisitions Efforts
Airline's Struggle to Survive
Oil & Gas Regulatory Compliance
Poorly Formulated Internet Initiatives
Attempt to Use Technology to Solve a Political Issue
Pride of Ownership Gets In the Way of Improvement
Best-of-Breed versus Enterprise-wide Philosophy
Farmer
Get in the Wheelbarrow
Build Your House on the Work Site
In a Heartbeat I Would
Five-Year Opportunity Plan
Defining the Opportunity
Assessing the Obligation
Beyond Organizational Boundaries
Scope within an Individual Function
Contingency Planning can have Ancillary Benefit
Scientist
Jargon Stifles Business Opportunity
Technical People can Eliminate Jargon Too
Poor Planning Wastes Time, Effort, and Money
Begin with Simple—Progress to Complex
Artist
Artists may be more lenient
Address Culture to Reduce Risk
Communication without Action Doesn't Work
Creativity should not be Limited to the Project Team
Corporate Mavericks as Advocates
Similar Situations—Different Approaches

Generalized Sequence of Tasks
Below, find a generalized sequence of when the tasks might occur for a PBC. A similar list of tasks is also provided here, sorted by their order of appearance in the book. This list, numbered 1 through 51 represents the most likely sequence the tasks would be performed.

    1. Prepare the Team (Farmer-Opportunity)
    2. Make a Vision Statement (Farmer-Opportunity)
    3. Find Business Opportunity (Farmer-Opportunity)

4. Define Scope (Farmer-Outcome)
5. List Cost and Benefit (Farmer-Obligation)
6. Quantify Cost and Benefit (Farmer-Obligation)
7. Clarify the Objectives (Farmer-Objectives)
8. Give the Project a Name (Artist-Communication)
9. Adopt a Methodology and Team Process (Scientist-Process)
10. Create a List of Project Goals (Farmer-Objectives)
11. Identify the Stakeholders (Artist-Communication)
12. Make a Communication Plan (Artist-Communication)
13. Make a Project Plan (Scientist-Plan)
14. Get Management Approval (Farmer-Outcome)
15. Discover the Issues (Scientist-Problems)
16. Create a Contingency Plan (Farmer-Order)
17. Learn About the People (Artist-Culture)
18. List Main Features of the Change (Scientist-Problems)
19. Make a Marketing Plan (Scientist-Plan)
20. Make a Supply Chain/Logistics Plan (Scientist-Plan)
21. Get More People on the Team (Artist-Creativity)
22. Outline Business Processes (Scientist-Process)
23. Draft User Wish List (Artist-Creativity)
24. Coordinate Departments (Artist-Creativity)
25. Promote the Project (Farmer-Opportunity)
26. List Basic Job Functions (Artist-Core HR)
27. Identify Job Relationships (Artist-Core HR)
28. Make a Prototype (Scientist-Prototype)
29. Draft Job Descriptions (Artist-Core HR)
30. Design Celebrations and Symbols (Artist-Culture)
31. Try out the Prototype (Scientist-Prototype)
32. Find Organization Design Opportunity (Artist-Core HR)
33. Write Procedures and Policies (Scientist-Process)
34. Demonstrate the Change (Artist-Creativity)
35. Advertise Test Results (Scientist-Prototype)
36. Draft Training Material (Artist-Capability)
37. Define Training Program (Artist-Capability)
38. Make a Scorecard (Scientist-Prudence)
39. Counsel the Stakeholder Groups (Artist-Creativity)
40. Identify Human Resource Programs (Artist-Core HR)
41. Finalize Training Material (Artist-Capability)
42. Make Job Aids (Artist-Capability)
43. Keep up the Communication (Artist-Communication)
44. Get Approval to Implement (Farmer-Order)

45. Deliver Training (Artist-Capability)
46. Put in Procedures (Scientist-Process)
47. Provide Follow-up Support (Scientist-Prudence)
48. Monitor the Change (Scientist-Prudence)
49. Examine Business Results (Farmer-Outcome)
50. Have a Celebration (Artist-Culture)
51. Respond to Organization Transition Issues (Artist-Culture)

Sequence of Tasks in this Book

Below, find the sequence the tasks occur within this book. They are grouped according to their primary associated role. A similar list of tasks is also provided sorted by the most likely sequence the tasks would be performed during a PBC, numbered 1 through 51. This list provides a convenient way to scan the tasks, grouped within the primary roles of Farmer, Scientist, and Artist.

Farmer-Opportunity
- Prepare the Team
- Make a Vision Statement
- Find Business Opportunity
- Promote the Project

Farmer-Obligation
- List Cost and Benefit
- Quantify Cost and Benefit

Farmer-Objectives
- Clarify the Objectives
- Create a List of Project Goals

Farmer-Outcome
- Define Scope
- Get Management Approval
- Examine Business Results

Farmer-Order
- Create a Contingency Plan
- Get Approval to Implement

Scientist-Plan
- Make a Project Plan
- Make a Marketing Plan
- Make a Supply Chain/Logistics Plan

Scientist-Problems
- List Main Features of the Change
- Discover the Issues

Scientist-Process

- Adopt a Methodology and Team Process
- Outline Business Processes
- Write Procedures and Policies
- Put in Procedures

Scientist-Prototype

- Make a Prototype
- Try out the Prototype
- Advertise Test Results

Scientist-Prudence

- Make a Scorecard
- Monitor the Change
- Provide Follow-up Support

Artist-Culture

- Learn About the People
- Design Celebrations and Symbols
- Have a Celebration
- Respond to Organization Transition Issues

Artist-Communication

- Identify the Stakeholders
- Make a Communication Plan
- Give the Project a Name
- Keep up the Communication

Artist-Creativity

- Get More People on the Team
- Coordinate Departments
- Draft User Wish List
- Demonstrate the Change
- Counsel the Stakeholder Groups

Artist-Capability

- Define Training Program
- Draft Training Material
- Finalize Training Material
- Make Job Aids
- Deliver Training

Artist-Core HR

- List Basic Job Functions
- Identify Job Relationships

- Draft Job Descriptions
- Find Organization Design Opportunity
- Identify Human Resource Programs

Trademarks, Service Marks, Copyrights and Credits

Credits: Cover by Photographer: Hemera Technologies. © 2005 Jupiter Images Corporation. ablestock image 23085931.

Accenture® is a registered trademark of Accenture Global Services GmbH CORPORATION SWITZERLAND Herrenacker 15 CH-8200 Schaffhausen SWITZERLAND

Capability Maturity Model® is a registered trademark of Carnegie Mellon University NOT-FOR-PROFIT CORPORATION PENNSYLVANIA 5000 Forbes Avenue Pittsburgh PENNSYLVANIA 15213

Malcolm Baldrige National Quality Award™ is a registered trademark of MALCOLM BALDRIGE NATIONAL QUALITY AWARD CONSORTIUM, INC., THE WISCONSIN P.O. BOX 443 MILWAUKEE WISCONSIN.

Provocative Business Change™ and Business-Turfing™ are trademarks in progress by John A. Honeycutt.

Part 10

Contact and Feedback

Contact Information

Your feedback, ideas, and constructive critique are welcome. Contact methods are described at www.businessturfing.com.

Thank you.

John.